Building Your Child's
SELF-
ESTEEM

Building Your Child's
SELF-ESTEEM

A Guide for LDS Parents

James M. Harris
with Kenneth A. Macnab

Bookcraft • Salt Lake City, Utah

Library of Congress Catalog Card Number: 83-71871
ISBN O-88494-500-6

3rd Printing, 1987

Lithographed in the United States of America
PUBLISHERS PRESS
Salt Lake City, Utah

Contents

1 Introduction   1

2 Teach Your Child About His
Divine Origin and Destiny   7

3 Boost Your Child's Feelings of Importance   12

4 Encourage Your Child to Do Things for Himself   19

5 Teach Your Child to Value and to Serve Others   27

6 Help Your Child to Give Love and Receive Love   36

7 Treat Your Child With Courtesy
and Consideration   42

8 Care Enough to Discipline Your Child   48

9 Spend Quality Time With Your Child   55

10 Let Your Child Make His Own Decisions   62

11 Give Your Child Freedom to Express
Negative Feelings   74

12 Encourage Creativity in Your Child   82

13 Take Time for Training   91

14 Conclusion   99

Index   103

Introduction 1

No opinion or judgment a person holds is as important as the view he has of himself. Children with high self-esteem view the world with optimism, confidence, and the expectation of success. Children with low self-esteem distrust their own abilities and approach life situations with insecurity, fear, and an expectation of failure.

Children who do not like themselves are apt to dislike others as well, and these feelings are reflected in their behavior. They may withdraw and feel sorry for themselves; or they may reach out aggressively and try to take by force what they do not know how to get in a better way. Children who continually and seriously misbehave are almost certain to be lacking in self-esteem.

The Parents' Role in Self-esteem

How can LDS parents help their children to develop self-esteem? The two main ingredients of self-worth are feelings of lovability and feelings of capability. To the degree that these feelings are present, a child's self-esteem is enhanced; to the degree that they are lacking, his self-esteem is severely threatened. We need to be sure, then, that in our interactions with our children we use techniques and communications that let them know we love them deeply and we see them as persons of great value.

Though the intentions of most parents are the very best, all of us are subject to normal human errors. We cannot hope to always say and do the thing that is best for each child at every given moment. Isn't it comforting to know that we do not always have to be right in order to raise normal, healthy children? God allows us to become good parents in spite of our human weaknesses. A child is more like a rubber ball then a china dish. He can bounce back again and again without breaking. But even a rubber ball can be mistreated to the point that it becomes shabby, worn, and unsightly and fails to bounce "true" anymore. Some children are so damaged by neglect or abuse that they also "lose their bounce" and become unattractive to themselves and others.

You may be a parent who is suspicious of books that tell how to raise children. If so, we sympathize with you. Different authors sometimes give conflicting advice. In a sense there are no "experts" in the complicated task of being a parent, and many times your own intuition and knowledge of your child will be more valuable than any book. But we believe that if you will give this book a chance and will apply the principles that it advocates, in combination with your own knowledge, experience, intuition, and inspiration from God, you will be a better parent and your children's self-esteem wil be enhanced.

Self-esteem and Conceit

Mike, age fifteen, has the reputation of being very con-ceited. At home he is often seen admiring his own reflection in the mirror. At school he loves to "lord it over" the other kids and often bullies children who are smaller or younger than he. He constantly puts others down and thinks that his opinion is the only correct one.

Is Mike an example of a child with too much self-esteem? Most likely just the opposite is true. Noisy conceit is often a way of covering up low self-esteem. A child with a high sense of his own value has no need to push others around—especially those who are too little or too weak to fight back. Vanity is more of a mark of low self-esteem than of high self-esteem, and if Mike really had high self-regard he would not need to resort to the constant reassurance of looking at himself in the mirror.

Self-esteem is a feeling of self-worth—a quiet sense of self-respect. A person with a genuine feeling of self-esteem has no need to cut others down in order to make himself feel important. Rather, he has an increased capacity to lift up those around him.

Self-esteem in a Gospel Perspective

If nothing else, a knowledge of who we are should generate self-esteem in Church members. One of the authors saw an elementary school child wearing a T-shirt with the inscription across the chest, "I must be good, 'cause God don't make no junk." Though the idea is expressed in a humorous way, the message is true and important. As spirit children of our Father in Heaven, we have within us the potential to become more and more like him. In a sense when we see ourselves as worthless and unlovable, we denigrate God himself.

How we feel about ourselves often relates to how we feel about other of our Father's children. The biblical injunction "Thou shalt love thy neighbour as thyself" (Matthew 19:19) does not mean that a person must be self-demeaning, or that he must lower his concept of himself to correspond with a low regard for others. Conversely, it means that a person should have a healthy and strong self-concept and also see those around him as persons of equal worth.

Enhancing Self-esteem in Children

Why does one child have sublime self-confidence and a high level of self-esteem and another child lack these attributes? The answer is not simple, and many factors are involved. Parents cannot assume all of the credit for a child's high self-esteem, nor need they accept all the blame for his low self-esteem. Nonetheless, child-rearing practices do exert a strong influence upon children's self-esteem. The following suggestions will help LDS parents to enhance self-esteem in their children:

1. *Teach your children about their spiritual beginnings and divine destiny.* Continually express the truth that just as they were created in our Father's physical image, they have the power within them to gradually grow in the direction of his spiritual image. Convince them that God loves them and wants them to succeed.

2. *Boost your child's feelings of importance.* Concentrate on strengths and positive attributes, not on weaknesses. Avoid comparisons with brothers and sisters. Teach him how both to win and to lose graciously.

3. *Encourage your child to do things for himself rather than to rely too much on others.* Our expectations for our children need to be realistic. Expecting too much or expecting too little of a child can be destructive to self-esteem.

4. *Teach your child to value and to serve others.* Looking for the good in others is often a natural step toward finding the good in oneself. When a person gives too much thought and attention to his own needs, it makes him self-centered and works against true self-esteem. The old saying "Whom we serve we love" is very appropriate. As your children do things for other people they develop love for those whom they serve, and their own feelings of self-worth blossom.

5. *Teach your child to give love and to receive love.* The best way to teach this lesson is to openly express your love for the child, both in word and action, and to do so consistently and often. Being with parents who love each other provides a good model. Nothing is so important to self-esteem as the feeling of being loved.

6. *Treat your child with courtesy and consideration.* If children are treated with kindness and consideration, they learn to think of themselves as persons of value. If they are treated with disrespect and if parents expect the worst of them, they are likely to behave badly and to have feelings of low self-

worth. We need to be as polite and considerate of our children as we are of our best friends.

7. *Care enough to discipline your child.* Allowing the child to do whatever he wants to do and not correcting his poor behavior is interpreted by the child as: "Mom and Dad must not really care very much about me or they would see that I do the right things."

8. *Spend quality time with your child.* We live in a busy world, and it sometimes seems there are not enough hours in the day to do all that needs to be done. It is sad that sometimes our children are the ones who are neglected. We need to make time for our children first—not try to squeeze in a few moments for them between our busy activities. Let your child know that he is important to you by spending time with him and his self-esteem will be enhanced.

9. *Encourage your child to trust his own ideas and make his own decisions.* Parents tend to make decisions for children long after they are capable of deciding for themselves. Allowing a child to make appropriate decisions contributes to his feelings of capability. The child thinks: "Hey! Mom and Dad trust my judgment and think I'm smart enough to decide for myself. I must be okay."

10. *Allow your child to express negative feelings.* "Bottled-up" emotions may fester and linger; expressed feelings are dissipated much more quickly. Furthermore, not to allow such expressions closes the lines of communication and makes it more difficult to know our children's thoughts and feelings, thus making it difficult to know how best to help them.

11. *Encourage creativity in your child.* A child who lacks self-confidence stays with activities that are "safe." He is reluctant to try anything new because of a fear of failure. Success in creative endeavor builds self-confidence and a willingness to accept the risk of trying out new things and adds to your child's feelings of capability and self-worth.

12. *Take time for training.* Tasks that seem clear-cut and simple to an adult may be confusing and overwhelming to a child. It is important for you to provide training so that your

children will perform assigned tasks well and develop feelings of capability and self-esteem.

This list of suggestions for enhancing self-esteem in children does not cover all possibilities, nor would it be practical to attempt to have it do so. But if you will make a conscientious effort to apply as many of these twelve suggestions as possible, your children's self-esteem is almost certain to be enhanced.

Summary

This introductory chapter stresses the importance of self-esteem and discusses the contribution that it makes to a child's success and happiness. Self-esteem is defined and contrasted with conceit or braggadocio. To have self-esteem, your child must believe he is lovable and capable. Twelve suggestions for building self-esteem have been presented and discussed briefly. A separate chapter of the book is devoted to each of these suggestions, with ideas for implementation and with practical examples.

Teach Your Child About His Divine Origin and Destiny

2

"What is man, that thou art mindful of him? and the son of man, that thou visitest him? For thou hast made him a little lower than the angels, and hast crowned him with glory and honour."

(Psalm 8:4-5.)

God is our Father, and we are his children. Some theologians would insist that the term *father* is used only in the sense of "creator," as we speak of the father of a painting or a musical composition. This view would say that man is no different from other animals, that he is a creation of God in the same sense that everything in the world is a product of his creation. But Latter-day Saints know that the term *father* as applied to God means "procreator." God is the father of the spirit in each human body in the same sense that the earthly father is the father of that body.

God is infinitely concerned about each one of his children. He is capable of a love that even surpasses the love that we have for our children, difficult though that may be for us to comprehend. Christ tells us that even the hairs on our head are numbered to God and that not even a sparrow falls without his knowledge (Matthew 10:29-30). We need to explain to our children that if God even knows when a sparrow falls, how much more concerned is he about each of his children! Though we cannot see or hear him, he knows us well. Furthermore, he loves each of us deeply and wants us to be happy and successful.

Can We Become Like God?

Just as a child can mature and develop the traits and characteristics of an earthly parent, he can eventually develop the traits and characteristics of a heavenly parent. In the Sermon on the Mount, Christ admonished, "Be ye therefore perfect, even as your Father which is in heaven is perfect" (Matthew 5:48). (In a footnote the new LDS Bible explains that for the word *perfect* as here used an alternate translation from the Greek is "complete, finished, fully developed.") Such perfection, though difficult to develop, must be possible to attain, otherwise Christ would not set up that goal for us. And while we cannot expect in this life to become perfect as the Father is perfect, we will never become so unless we do all we can in that direction while in mortality. Our children need to know that eternity has already begun and that God expects us to make regular progress in improving our lives and blessing the lives of others. Because God loves us deeply, he will help us to develop those attributes that will lead us to perfection.

We have been instructed to love God with all our heart, mind, and strength, and to love our neighbor as ourselves. If our children really understand the concept of the fatherhood of God and the brotherhood of man, they will be able to see the necessity of treating all of our Father's children with kindness and consideration. And as they learn to value others, they will also learn to value themselves.

Humility and Self-esteem

Latter-day Saints are continually admonished to be humble and meek. Christ said, "Blessed are the meek: for they shall inherit the earth" (Matthew 5:5). In following verses of the same chapter the Savior admonished his followers not to resist evil—meaning not to retaliate. In fact, he said, if any should strike one of them on the right cheek, he should turn the other cheek for the attacker to strike; if any were to sue one of them at the law and take away his coat, he should also give the other person his cloak; and if someone were to compel one of them to carry a burden a mile, he should voluntarily go a second mile. Such advice would be thought irrational and totally ridiculous by those of the world. It is even hard for us to comprehend this advice. How could we be so self-demeaning and at the same time maintain our self-respect?

It would seem that a person's motivation in not retaliating would be all-important. If a person fails to strike back because of fear, there would presumably be no merit to the behavior. But if the lack of retaliation is based on love rather than on fear, it is meritorious indeed. Christ said, "Love your enemies, bless them that curse you, do good to them that hate you, and pray for them which despitefully use you, and persecute you; that ye may be the children of your Father which is in heaven" (Matthew 5:44-45). He followed his own advice, when on the cross he said, "Father, forgive them; for they know not what they do" (Luke 23:34). Lest we think that only Jesus, because of his inherent Godhood, could pray for his enemies at the very time they were mocking him and putting him to death, let us remember Stephen. While being stoned to death, he was able to pray, "Lord, lay not this sin to their charge" (Acts 7:60).

If we can develop the love that Jesus would have us develop for all mankind, even our enemies, we can resist evil out of love rather than out of fear. A missionary and his companion in a European country introduced themselves to a man who came to the door. Without warning, the man hit one of the missionaries with a brutal blow that knocked him down the stairs. Surely the temptation must have been great for that missionary, who was much bigger than the man who had struck him, to retaliate, if not physically then at least with unkind words. But as the missionary pulled himself up from the ground, he expressed love for the man and sorrow that he was not willing to listen to the very important message that the Lord had sent them to deliver to him. The missionaries then left.

Years later the missionary related the incident in a talk. After the meeting a man came up to him and with tears in his eyes said that he was the man who had struck him. Because of the way the missionary had reacted to his unkindness, the man had become ashamed of his behavior and had listened to the next missionaries who came to his door.

If we sincerely heeded the advice of Jesus to love our enemies, soon we would have no enemies. As we learn to discipline our own behavior and to love all of our Father's children, we enhance our feelings of lovability, capability, and self-esteem.

Examples of Self-esteem

Throughout the centuries the Lord has worked through prophets whom he called to do his work on the earth. In many cases they were called in their youth, while they were still teachable. Many of them were surprised and could not understand why they had been singled out. Moses told the Lord that he was "slow of speech" (Exodus 4:10). Many of those he called wondered why they had been chosen in place of others who were older, wiser, and more experienced. But the Lord knew their hearts and minds, and they became effective instruments in his hands. In spite of their modesty and wonderment at being selected, these were men of high self-esteem. Could a person who lacked a sense of self-worth have the confidence to lead the children of Israel out of Egypt? to build an ark? to become a ruler in Egypt? to lead multitudes into battle? to return to Jerusalem to get the brass plates of Laban? to go up to battle against a giant? to march around the city of Jericho, having faith that the Lord would bring down the walls?

Jesus Christ himself is perhaps the best example of one who combined self-esteem and humility. He washed the Apostles' feet; yet he was bold in declaring himself the Son of Man, Jehovah, the Savior and Redeemer of the world. From at least the age of twelve, when he confronted the doctors and wise men in the temple, Jesus knew of his divine Sonship and his divine destiny. We too and our children need to believe in our own divine destinies and to comprehend the full extent of our divine worth.

Elder Hugh B. Brown told the story of how, as a young officer in the Canadian army, he found himself at a party at which various forms of debauchery were taking place. Only he and one other officer were not participating in these activities. Elder Brown turned to the other officer and asked why he was not involved in what was going on. The man replied that he would never allow himself to behave in that way because he was a member of the royal household of England. This caused Elder Brown to ponder: that he himself could not behave that way, because he was a member of royalty—the royal priesthood of God.

Our feelings of self-esteem are enhanced when we really understand who we are and when we act in accordance with the revealed truths we have received. How important it is for our children to know that they also are members of a royal family and a holy priesthood! Such knowledge will help them to avoid sin and debauchery and the guilt feelings and loss of self-esteem such behavior produces.

Summary

We are God's children, and he loves each one of us deeply. He wants us to be happy and successful. Our children need to see perfection as their long-range goal; however, they should not be too discouraged or give up because of setbacks along the way. Humility is not incompatible with self-esteem. Without positive feelings of self-worth we would not have the courage to meet the challenges that life has to offer.

Boost Your Child's Feelings of Importance

3

"For as he thinketh in his heart, so is he"
(Proverbs 23:7).

Many years ago Dale Carnegie wrote a best-seller entitled *How to Win Friends and Influence People.* Few books have had greater impact in teaching effective principles of persuasion and influence. One of Carnegie's suggestions is that we visualize each person we meet as wearing a sign across the chest saying, *"I want to be important."* What good advice! Yet how seldom we act upon it! If we will consistently employ this technique as we interact with our children, we will act in ways that help them to feel important and that enhance their self-esteem.

Emphasize the Positive, Ignore the Negative

Not all children are equally attractive, intelligent, or capable. But all of God's children, our spirit brothers and sisters, have merit and worth. Parental reactions have much to do with how a child perceives himself and how confidently he faces the world. An LDS mother living in an attractive, well-kept home referred to one of her children as "really dumb." This remark to a visitor was made in the child's presence. A very real danger here is that the child will simply accept herself as "really dumb" and behave accordingly.

There is a somewhat natural tendency for a parent to call a child's attention to negative behavior and bad traits in an attempt to change the child for the better. The trouble is that, more often than not, it doesn't work. Emphasizing the negative tends to cause either anger or anxiety, and in either case the bad behavior tends to be reinforced instead of weakened or eliminated.

It is far better to call your child's attention to his positive traits and behavior than to criticize him for his negative ones. Such positive attention helps your child to feel good about both you and himself, and it gives him a feeling of importance and self-worth. As you at the same time ignore the bad features, they will tend to slip quietly away.

When your child completes a task, the natural tendency is to point out the weak areas so that he will improve next time. However, to do so is often to discourage your child and make him less willing to try again. It is much better to comment on the parts of the performance that were done well and perhaps not even mention the mistakes.

Suppose your son is put to work painting your fence, and he does some parts well and others quite carelessly. What will happen if you say: "I should have known I couldn't trust you to do a decent job! Look how the paint has run on this board! And you can see the old color shining through on this one!" How willing do you think your boy will be to try next time you have a painting job for him?

Put yourself in a similar situation. If the reader is a woman, suppose you have spent the entire day cleaning the house, and it shines from top to bottom—except for one room you didn't have time to get to. Or, if the reader is a man, suppose you have weeded the entire garden—except for one small section. How would it make you feel if your spouse were to say: "Boy, the sewing room is a mess. How can you stand to work in all that clutter?" Or, "I was just out in the carrot patch, and I couldn't find the carrots for all the weeds!" Would such statements make you want to rush right back and complete the job, or would you feel some resentment and hostility?

Back to the example of your son and the fence. Suppose you were to say: "I really appreciate the way you went right ahead on your own and finished the fence. I especially like these sections you painted so evenly, and no paint runs at all!" If you should use this approach, you might be surprised to see him sneak back to the fence, get out the paint and brush again, and redo the sections that were not done well. In any case, you protect his feelings of capability and self-esteem.

The Danger of Invidious Comparisons

Carl, the oldest boy in the family, has always been a good boy. He has never caused his parents a moment of trouble. He attends all his Church meetings regularly, is an officer in his Aaronic Priesthood quorum, and is on his way to being an Eagle Scout. Jim, two years younger than Carl, is another story. It seems to the parents that Jim is always into some kind of trouble. He has to be forced to go to church, and he thinks that Scouting is "stupid."

How can two boys in a family be so different? Part of Jim's problem is actually Carl. Jim sees little chance of outshining his brother for good attention, so he has unconsciously decided to get attention in other ways in an attempt to be "his own person." Unknowingly the parents are compounding the problem by constantly calling Jim's attention to his inadequacies with statements, such as "Why can't you be more like Carl?" or, "If you'd work a little harder, you might be able to do almost as well as Carl."

It is not uncommon for parents to compare a child in an unfavorable way with another child in the family. Often the parents' motivation is the very best — to set up a positive example for the child. But it is really unfair to expect a child, with his own unique set of characteristics, to compete with a brother or sister who may have quite different attributes.

Sometimes invidious comparisons are made openly, with statements such as those mentioned above. But often the comparison is made in a very subtle way without the parent even being aware that such a comparison has been made. But in either case the message is clear: "I am not as lovable or as capable as my brother or sister."

It is hard enough for a child to try to live up to the example of an older sibling. But it is especially galling to have a younger child put up on a pedestal. In considering the story of Joseph who was sold into Egypt, we usually look at things from his point of view. But did you ever find yourself feeling some empathy for his ten older brothers? From the beginning Joseph was his father's favorite because he was born to Jacob's favorite wife. He was singled out and granted preferential treatment, and his father gave him a beautiful coat of many colors. Is it any wonder that his brothers both hated and envied him? Finally, when he had the temerity to tell them that he had had a dream in which he saw his brothers bow down to him, it was more than they could bear. Given their tempestuous spirits, it is little wonder that they tore up his beautiful coat, threw him into a pit, and sold him into bondage in Egypt.

Sometimes it is the child who makes the negative comparison between himself and his brother or sister. When this occurs, he needs to have the assurance that he enjoys the same love from his parents as does the competing child. He also needs to be loved just for himself—not for what he can or cannot do. At the same time he needs to begin to develop his own talents. Parents should bring to his attention skills and talents he may not recognize, emphasize that everyone has unique abilities, and encourage him to develop his own abilities rather than to compete with his brothers and sisters.

Highlight Your Child's Accomplishments

When Mark makes an achievement in school, at church, or in Scouting, both parents make it a point to be there, regardless of what other commitments they have. But his friend Max's parents are usually too busy to come to such events. They do not think that their presence at Courts of Honor or at school programs is really all that important. What an opportunity Max's parents are missing in not supporting their son's activities! To do so would help him to feel important and enhance his self-esteem.

You should praise your children's accomplishments. But a note of caution is in order. The praise you give must always be sincere. Children are quick to detect insincere compliments.

Make Opportunities for Your Child to Win

A parent asks, "Should I deliberately lose at games sometimes so that my child can experience success and a feeling of competency?" We believe that parents should let the child win sometimes. It will not be much fun for him to play games in which he is never the winner, and he may feel discouraged or incompetent. But the older the child, the more difficult it is to let him win without his knowing what is happening; and trying to fool him into thinking he beat you when he really didn't may have negative consequences.

Another approach is to switch to games wherein chance, rather than memory and experience, is the main dimension. In this type of game your child will automatically win for his share of the time, and you will not have to deliberately let him win.

It is always fun to win, but your children must learn that no one wins all the time. He needs to be able to lose without it affecting his self-concept. Let's face it! If mom and dad always lose, they may begin to appear quite inept; and inept parents is not the image we hope to create with our children.

Some parents find little joy in competitive activities if they have to deliberately lose in order to help their children to develop self-esteem. Jim Anderson is that kind of man. So he has developed ways of giving a son or daughter a handicap without the child knowing that he has the head start. Steve, his fourteen-year-old son, loves to go to the gym with his dad to practice shooting the basketball and play some "one-on-one." For his age the boy has become an excellent shooter. Because of Jim's height and experience, he could probably win in a game of "twenty-one" every time. He could guard his son very closely and block most of his shots if he wanted to go all out to win. What he does is to guard his son closely enough that he does not get unmolested shots at the basket, but not so closely that he cannot get off his shots. Jim's own shots are taken far enough away from the basket to be almost beyond his range, so that he does not make a high percentage. If his son begins to get a few baskets ahead, the father will try a few lay-ups or close-in shots to catch up. If the father gets a little ahead, he will try a left-handed hook shot or one from almost midcourt. But he never deliberately misses a shot at the basket. Who wins the game is often a matter of who happens to hit the last basket.

Jim Anderson uses a similar approach in playing Ping-Pong with his ten-year-old daughter. He does it, not by deliberately missing the table, but by playing left-handed. So far the daughter has not even noticed his subterfuge. When she finally notices that dad plays with her with his left hand, he will simply tell her that since he has had twenty or so more years of experience at Ping-Pong than she, it seems fair to even up the odds a bit.

You may wish to try the technique Jim Anderson uses. All too soon you may find that you no longer need to give your child a handicap; in fact, you may have to put forth an all-out effort to win your share of the games.

Laugh With Your Children, Not at Them

A sense of humor is a real asset to a parent, or to any adult who interacts with children. This does not necessarily mean that you should constantly tell your child jokes. But to be able to see the humor in situations that arise and laugh with your child can promote a feeling of camaraderie and dispel feelings of tension. But it is important that you laugh *with* your child, not *at* him. When a person, especially a child, sees someone laughing at him, he receives a blow to his self-esteem.

Tammy and four other girls from her Primary class sang "I Am a Child of God" in sacrament meeting. They sang very well, but their sweet voices and angelic faces caused a titter of laughter in the congregation. When Tammy got home from church she asked her mother: "Why did people laugh at us? Didn't we sing well?" Another child, George, gave a short talk on the occasion of his graduation from Primary. When he made a minor error by using a word incorrectly, some members of the congregation again laughed. George's face flushed in embarrassment, and he vowed to himself not to talk in church again for a good long time.

Lori and her family, while driving through the countryside, came to a lake. The little six-year-old girl asked in all seriousness if that was the ocean. This question caused her older brother and sister to laugh at her, and even mom and dad joined in the fun. Their laughter caused Lori to feel stupid and unimportant. Mom and dad thought the question was "cute" and repeated it to their friends, and again Lori was embarrassed. Experiences such as this were repeated on other occasions, and Lori became reluctant to ask questions for fear of ridicule. Furthermore, there was a negative impact upon her self-esteem.

Parents need to be careful to prevent such incidents of ridicule and embarrassment and to handle situations in such a way as to help the child save face. Instead of joining in the laughter of their older children, Lori's parents should have made comments to the effect that this was a very natural question for a child of her age.

Summary

In this chapter we have discussed ways in which you can help your child feel important. Highlight his *own* accomplishments and avoid comparisons with brothers and sisters. Sincerely praise his achievements and emphasize the positive aspects of what he does rather than the weaknesses. Provide experiences in which he can win for his share of the time, but also teach him to lose without it adversely affecting his self-esteem. We concluded by suggesting that you laugh *with* your child, not *at* him.

Encourage Your Child to Do Things for Himself

"Verily I say, men should be anxiously engaged in a good cause, and do many things of their own free will... For the power is in them, wherein they are agents unto themselves."
(D&C 58:27-28.)

Children learn effectively when their readiness for a given concept or skill is well established. If we force learning too soon, interest in the activity may be lacking, and interest is one important ingredient of readiness. Other aspects of readiness, such as the child's physical maturation, may also be insufficiently developed when we start too early.

Just as we can force learning too early, it is also possible to delay learning for too long. The interest may lag, and the child may actually be less effective in his learning at that stage than he would have been earlier. For example, if a mother continues to feed a child completely up to eighteen months of age or so in order to avoid the mess that he would make in feeding himself, she runs the risk that he will stop trying to take the spoon out of her hand and be content to let her continue to wait on him unnecessarily.

Develop Realistic Expectations for Your Child

We often expect either too much or too little from our children, and either extreme is apt to cause low self-esteem. Sister Parks expects her two-year-old twins to sit through all of the Sunday meetings quietly. She does not believe in entertaining them with picture books or "snacks" and she becomes upset with them when they become restless or noisy. She feels that children need to be taught proper church behavior very early so as to build correct habits. Brother Thomas expects his son James, age eight, to fast a full twenty-four hours on fast day now that he has been baptized. In both cases the parents are expecting too much, and the lesson that is being learned more than any other may be the dislike of Church meetings and the lack of appreciation for Church principles.

John does not want to go to Scout camp. He and his family have recently moved into a new area, and John doesn't know the other boys in the troop. John's father places a high value on Scouting and was himself an Eagle Scout. He can't understand why his son would possibly not want to go to camp, and he uses mild ridicule and tells him not to be a crybaby in order to try to change his mind. The father does not seem to realize the negative effect he is having upon his son's feelings of capability and self-worth.

If we are never quite satisfied with the way our children perform expected tasks and continually do them over or point out how they should have been done, we discourage our children and make them feel that they are not capable of doing anything right. Such a feeling has a very negative impact upon the development of healthy self-esteem.

How can we develop realistic expectations for our children? There are at least four main ways:

1. *Compare your child with children his own age.* Child development specialists have done studies to determine what behaviors can be expected of children of every age from infancy through adolescence. We can find these norms in child-development books. For example, the average child learns to walk between the tenth and sixteenth month of life. By age three most normal children begin to put two or more words together to form simple sentences. Such information can be helpful; but remember that these statistics are based on averages, and some children will be ready sooner and some later. By comparing your child with other children in the

neighborhood of the same age, you can judge whether your child is a fast learner, an average learner, or a slow learner, and adjust your expectations accordingly. Even so, development may not be the same in every developmental area, and you will have to adjust expectations in terms of what you know about his strong and weak areas.

2. *Be alert to a natural order of development.* Children are much more alike in the *sequence* of development than in the *rate* of development. Most children crawl before they walk; they learn individual words before they put them together into phrases; they are able to go upstairs before they learn to go down them. By seeing where your child is in a given learning sequence, you can predict his readiness for further learnings in the same area.

3. *Watch for signs of interest in your child.* This is a very practical way for you to know when your child is at a point of readiness for a specific developmental task. When your child wants to take the spoon out of your hand, or to pick up the food with his hands, he is ready to learn to feed himself. When he becomes interested in the toilet and aware of his own bowel movements, it is a good time to begin toilet training.

When your four-year-old daughter wants to "help" you do the dishes, don't say, "Sorry, sweetie, but you're really too little." When your six-year-old son wants to "help" you paint the fence, don't say, "No, you'll get paint all over you and everything else." Find the most simple aspect of dishwashing and let her do it even though it takes longer to finish the job. Tie one of your worn-out shirts around your son and let him paint. Neither child is likely to persist for more than a very few minutes anyway, but for the time being you have fostered feelings of capability rather than discouraged them. When their interest lags, thank them sincerely for their help and compliment them for what they have done.

4. *Consult professional help when questions arise.* If any area of development causes you real concern, consult a person who is trained to recognize and remedy problems in that area. If you suspect a sensory defect or any other kind of physical

problem, consult a physician. If you have serious concerns about how your child relates to other children, or about how he feels inside, consult a school psychologist or counselor. More often than not you will find that you have been overly concerned and that your child is within normal limits, but at least you will be able to relax and allay your anxiety. If there really is a problem, to procrastinate a decision to seek professional help may allow it to become increasingly serious and difficult to remedy.

Allow Your Child to Explore His World

Children are naturally curious and inquisitive. Parents should be happy to see these traits develop in their children; but too often the parents are threatened or irritated instead, because of the trouble or inconvenience that can be caused by such curiosity and inquisitiveness.

For example, Richard, age fourteen months, is placed in his high chair and given oatmeal, banana slices, and milk for breakfast. He accidentally drops his spoon over the side of the high-chair tray. Clunk! It hits the floor. Richard, finding the sound of the spoon hitting the floor to be intriguing, searches his tray for something else to drop—all in the name of science, naturally. While reaching for the banana slices he accidentally knocks over his "spill-proof" glass. Milk instantly dribbles down from the tray, splashing magically on the floor, individual drops coming together to form a puddle. Richard notices that the falling milk makes very little noise as it makes contact with the floor—quite different from the sound of the spoon.

Again, wondering what might be dropped next, his eyes settle on the bowl of oatmeal. Reaching his tiny hand into the bowl, he finds a nice squishy texture, much softer than the spoon. "I wonder what sound this will make?" With a glance to the floor he positions his hand and releases the missile. Down, down it falls—splat! What fun! And what a feeling of power for a fourteen-month-old!

Now, with nothing else on the tray to drop, our inquisitive child may change "curriculum" from sound production to tactile experimentation. He rubs his hand around in the cereal that is left in the tray and then over his face and hair. With a zestful feeling he next proceeds to coat his clothing and high chair as well. Mother, who has only been gone from the room for a minute or two, hears the squeals of ecstasy and enters the room—only to find a veritable disaster area. Finding it hard to hold back her anger, she retorts: "You naughty little boy! Look what a mess you've made for mother!" Yanking him from the chair, she holds him at arms' distance and whisks him off to the bathroom.

Richard, of course, had no way of knowing that his activities, so interesting to him, would be painful and irritating to his mother. If mother reacts by slapping his hands and speaking to him in a loud, harsh voice, she will only succeed in confusing him, since he does not know that his exploratory behavior was wrong nor understand why mother is angry. Though mom and dad are not apt to think of it in this way, Richard has been conducting scientific research and has been creating, learning, and growing in knowledge and experience.

The understanding mother who enters the kitchen to find that her young child has pulled out every pan and lid from the cupboard and strewn them over the kitchen floor recognizes that the child is not just messing up the house. The act is a result of curiosity and experimentation. She may have even left the cupboard door open on purpose to encourage such exploration.

Naturally there are some items in the home that you do not want your child to touch. While your child is too young to understand limits and proscriptions, you need to "childproof" your home by putting expensive and breakable objects out of reach. Of course you will also put caustic and hazardous items well out of reach. As the child becomes old enough to understand, you can train him to know which things are allowed and which are not. Your child should feel that it is his home too, and restrictions should be only those necessary to protect the child himself or objects of value.

Help Your Child to Develop Initiative and Courage to Face Life Situations

Feelings of independence and confidence can begin to develop in a child from a very early age—certainly by age three or four. Do not feel threatened when your child says, "Me do it!" Be grateful that he is exercising an intuitive drive to become "his own person." The process of setting a child free should be a very gradual one and should begin very early in life. The following are a few suggestions for helping children to develop initiative and build self-confidence:

1. *Do not do anything for your child that he can do for himself.* A parent who continually takes over and does things for a child that he could do for himself runs the risk of promoting dependency rather than self-reliance in the child. When we say to a child, "Oh, darling, you're much too small for this; let me help you," we encourage feelings of incompetence and aid erosion of self-esteem. A succession of such experiences may cause the child to distrust his own capabilities and to wait for the parents to do everything for him. Whenever we do things for children that they should be doing for themselves, we pay a price, and so do they. We use up time that could very likely be spent in a better way, and our children perceive that we see them as inept, thus adversely affecting their feelings of self-worth.

2. *Expect and allow mistakes.* We should not be so afraid that a child will make a mistake that we curtail his opportunities for practice. A mother may say to a four-year-old child: "Here, let me pour your milk for you, dear. You might spill it." The risk of spilling a little milk is a very small one compared to the value of conveying to the child that we see him as competent. If he should spill the milk, an excellent teaching opportunity arises as he helps mom or dad clean it up.

3. *Be patient and accept the child's performance at his level.* It is often easier to do something for a child than it is to allow him to do it for himself: "I'll make Mary's bed for her; it'll save time, and besides, I can't stand the sloppy way she makes it." "I always butter Mike's bread for him; I can't bear to watch him tear up his bread and butcher the butter cube." "I can do the dishes and the yard work much more efficiently and faster myself; the kids just get in the way." More often than not our children are all too willing to let us do all the work, and they may even feign ineptness to further encourage us to do so.

In the beginning stages do not expect your child to accomplish a task at your level of speed and accuracy. If the child has done his best, praise the effort and avoid the temptation to show how much better you can do it. Your twelve-year-old daughter may make her bed as well as you make yours (especially if you provided the necessary training when she was younger), and she may do so every day. But do not expect that same level of quality and consistency from her seven-year-old sister.

If you accept your children's efforts at their own levels of proficiency, they learn to trust their abilities, and they are likely to accept other responsibilities with self-confidence. Initiative and self-esteem are enhanced.

4. *Challenge your child early.* Parents sometimes underestimate the capabilities of young children. It is surprising what children can accomplish with a minimum amount of help and training from the parent.

Stevie, who just turned three, is a child of considerable self-esteem. Because his parents have encouraged him to do many things on his own, he feels capable. One day he decided he wanted to put his underpants on by himself. He watched his older brother and tried to imitate his method, but Stevie lacked the balance necessary to do it the way his brother did. So he came to his father for help. His father taught him to set the underpants on the floor, arrange them so the holes could be stepped into, and then grasp the elastic top and pull them up. It worked very well, and the child's face reflected the pride and satisfaction he felt in having mastered the task. In a similar way he has learned to get into the bathtub by himself and to wash his own hair with a minimum amount of help from his parents.

Often it is faster and more efficient for a parent to do something for the child than to wait for him to do it. But in the long run a great deal of the parents' time will be saved as the child becomes more and more self-sufficient.

Summary

Children, like a well-groomed garden or yard, do not just happen. They are a product of hard work and careful nurturing. We need to develop realistic expectations for our children, because our having expectations that are either too high or too low can negatively affect children's self-esteem. Child-development norms, though useful, only show what behavior is average for children of a given age. Each child is unique and presents an individual challenge. Attention to sequences of development and to the child's own interests provides clues as to when he is ready to learn specific things.

Allow your child the freedom and opportunity to explore his world. Avoid the temptation to do too much for him, as you may curtail his initiative and self-confidence and lower his self-esteem. Accept your child's performances at *his* level, and do not expect an adult level of competence. As you allow your child to do things for himself, his feelings of competency will grow and his self-esteem will be enhanced.

Teach Your Child to Value and to Serve Others

5

"By love serve one another. For all the law is fulfilled in one word, even in this; Thou shalt love thy neighbour as thyself."
(Galatians 5:13-14.)

About thirty years ago a missionary conference was held at Anadarko, Oklahoma, in the heart of Indian country. All the missionaries who were laboring in the state of Oklahoma were invited to be present. Presiding was a General Authority of the Church by the name of Spencer W. Kimball. At that time many of the choice Lamanite people were being converted to the gospel, and there was to be a baptismal service down at the river bank immediately following the conference session. As the meeting ended, the missionaries were asked to carry chairs down to the site of the baptismal service.

It was with surprise bordering on astonishment that members, investigators, and missionaries saw Elder Kimball begin to pick up more than his share of chairs and transport them to the area where they were needed. Many men in his situation, reasoning that there were plenty of young missionaries to carry chairs, would have visited with local authorities or members or found something else to do during the interim period. As I walked beside Elder Kimball, who was carrying chairs, I thought of the contrast with religious leaders who are adored and borne about on men's shoulders, and into my mind came the scripture "And whosoever will be chief among

you, let him be your servant: Even as the Son of man came not
to be ministered unto, but to minister, and to give his life a
ransom for many" (Matthew 20:27-28). No doubt to Elder
Kimball this incident was routine and not noteworthy, but for
more than thirty years it has remained in the mind of at least
one person as an example of humility and service.

Self-centeredness and Self-esteem

Think about a person you know who has a highly
developed sense of personal worth. What kind of a person is
he or she? Would you say that this person is very self-conscious, easily embarrassed, overly concerned about appear-
ances? Does this person continually talk about himself? try to
make himself appear better than others? Is he unconcerned
about others' feelings? vain and conceited? opinionated and
unwilling to listen to the ideas of others?

The probable answer to each of these questions is no. The
person with true self-esteem does not have to be constantly
thinking about himself. Rather, he is most likely the one who
can forget himself and lose himself in service to others. Christ
said, "He that findeth his life shall lose it: and he that loseth his
life for my sake shall find it" (Matthew 10:39). King Benjamin,
in his speech to the people of Zarahemla, said, "And behold, I
tell you these things that ye may learn wisdom; that ye may
learn that when ye are in the service of your fellow beings ye
are only in the service of your God" (Mosiah 2:17). A person
who has low self-esteem is limited in the extent to which he can
give thought and attention to others. He is so caught up in his
own needs that be becomes self-centered and unconcerned
about others.

There is a close relationship between a person's feelings
about others and his feelings about himself. Looking for the
good in others is a natural step toward finding the good in
one's self.

Teaching Children to Look for the Good in Others

What are some ways in which you as a parent can effectively teach your children to find good in other people? Let's
examine just a few:

1. *Be a good model for your child.* This is the most obvious and the most effective way to teach almost anything we want our children to learn. We need to minimize gossip and scandalous reports and to let our conversations about people be as positive as possible. One of the New Testament authors devotes almost an entire chapter of his book to a discussion of the power of the tongue (see James, chapter 3). He draws an analogy with the rudder of a ship, which, though it be very small in relation to the size of the vessel, is able to direct the ship wherever the person who holds the rudder wants it to go. Even so the tongue is very small in relation to the size of our bodies, and yet it exerts a powerful influence upon the directions that we take. "Out of the same mouth proceedeth blessing and cursing" (James 3:10).

Consider these bits of conversation overheard as elementary-aged children talked with their friends:

"I just hate President _____. He doesn't care at all about the poor people; all he cares about is the rich guys. I hope he doesn't get in again."

"The bishop doesn't pay any attention to the older people in the ward like my dad and mom; the only ones he cares about are the teenagers."

"I don't feel sorry for people on welfare. If they weren't so lazy, they'd go to work like my dad does and not expect everybody else to support 'em."

It's obvious where these children acquired their attitudes. To quote some words from a song in the musical *South Pacific*, "You've got to be taught to hate." Sometimes adults teach it directly; sometimes, in subtle ways. But in either case children learn the lesson very well.

2. *Correct misconceptions immediately.* The home is not always at fault. Children may acquire negative attitudes from schoolmates, teachers, and numerous other sources, including the mass media. If we keep the lines of communication open with our children, we can be aware of some of the false ideas they pick up and can work to correct them.

3. *Be selective in the books, movies, and television programs to which your children are exposed.* Never before in

the history of the world have children been exposed to such a variety of ideas and philosophies. Help your children to choose programs and stories that reflect human nature at its best, not at its worst.

4. *Teach the positive virtues of people of other cultures and nationalities.* Deemphasize the cultural stereotypes that present a given racial or ethnic group in negative ways. For example, we can talk about the musical and athletic abilities of Blacks, the beautiful art and rich culture of Spanish-Americans, and the family solidarity of the Japanese and Jewish peoples and the great value which both groups place on education. Invite people of minority groups to your home, and encourage your children to do the same.

5. *Accentuate the positive, ignore the negative.* If we are not careful, we can let negative things occupy too much of our time and attention. It seems that there is a natural human tendency to dwell on the bad things people do. Consider, for example, the average newspaper. Is it filled with stories of human courage, devotion, honor, kindness, and integrity? While you can find some human-interest stories that bring out the best in human nature, most of the space is devoted to human follies: crime, debauchery, conflict, unkindness, and dishonesty. It seems that it is the latter type of story that arouses attention and sells newspapers. It is important in our daily lives and in our interaction with our children that we maintain a positive outlook and that we focus attention upon the positive side of human behavior. Both we and our children need to know that the negative side of human nature, which is so often highlighted in the news and entertainment media, is overshadowed by the inherent goodness, integrity, and heroism which are displayed in a quiet way by people in the "real world."

6. *Use "reverse tattling" and "reverse gossiping."* Glenn A. Jorgenson, an LDS psychologist, has developed what he calls a Positive Action Theory of Behavior. He suggests that parents and teachers need to find positive ways of teaching and help-ing young people to develop good emotional health and

character. He notes that there is a strong human tendency to observe and report weaknesses in others. Any elementary teacher can attest to the truth of this observation. It is difficult to know the best way to handle tattling. Although the teacher or parent is often grateful to know the information that has been communicated, he must be careful to see that the child who tattles does not get rewarded for it, thus encouraging the tattling behavior to be repeated.

Jorgenson suggests that children be taught to say good things about each other: "If you can't say something nice, don't say anything at all."

Jorgenson also suggests that parents and teachers use "reverse tattling" and "reverse gossiping." Under these concepts, children report positive things they see other children doing. One of the authors is personally aware of an elementary school that promotes positive practices similar to those proposed by Jorgenson. Each week a "Good Guy" award is given, which includes, among other things, a certificate and a pen. Any child in the school can nominate any other child for the award, but of course no one can nominate himself. The child who nominates the winner for the week also gets some recognition himself. In this way children get in the habit of looking for good things they can report about each other.

7. *Teach your children to give sincere compliments and to accept compliments graciously.* For some reason criticizing others seems to come to children (and to adults) more easily than complimenting does. Yet compliments are infinitely more effective in correcting and maintaining desired behavior. As you help people to feel better about themselves, they also feel better toward you; and the self-esteem of both is enhanced.

Teach Your Children the Joy of Service

"It is more blessed to give than to receive" (Acts 20:35), said the Apostle Paul, reinforcing the teachings of Jesus. It is an interesting phenomenon that when one person gives to another, whether it be tangible goods or benevolent service, it is often the benefactor rather than the recipient who develops the stronger feelings of love and affection. Certainly the act of giving inherently generates more self-esteem than does the act of taking. As we teach our children to find pleasure in helping others, we also see a definite by-product, that is, growth in their feelings of self-worth.

What are some effective ways of teaching children to serve others? Let us suggest just a few:

1. *Teach children to play good tricks on others rather than bad ones.* There is a well-known story of two boys who saw a man fishing down by a river. One of the boys noted that the man had taken off his shoes, and he suggested that they play a trick on him by hiding his shoes. But his friend, pointing out that the man was shabbily dressed and probably poor, suggested that rather than hide his shoes they put a silver dollar in each one. So they sneaked down quietly and put a dollar in each shoe. Then they retreated to a place where they could watch the man unobserved. Soon he gathered his things together and prepared to leave. As he put on each shoe he felt the dollars; and when he found out what they were, he was overjoyed. He immediately fell to his knees, offered up a prayer of thanks to God, and expressed gratitude that now his children would have food to eat that night. Think how much better these two young men felt than they would have had the original plan of hiding the shoes been followed!

2. *Encourage your children to do good deeds anonymously.* This idea is taken from Jorgenson's Positive Action Theory of Behavior, mentioned earlier in this chapter. He suggests that we give children opportunities to "practice doing something nice without getting caught." Let's think of how this might work in an actual family situation. Suppose two of your children are having some problems in relating to one another, and there are some ill feelings between them. One of them tells you that he feels like going into the other one's room and taking or destroying one of his possessions. As you quietly talk with your child and let him ventilate his feelings, you suggest that instead of following his natural feelings of hurting the

other child, he secretly do something good for him instead, such as polishing his shoes or leaving a treat on his dresser.

It may not be easy to convince the child to do something nice for his "enemy," especially while the emotional feelings are still high. But if and when he does finally agree, the results are almost sure to be beneficial. You and the child can secretly enjoy the befuddlement of the other child as he tries to determine the identity of his secret pal. The very act of doing something good for the other child will lead to more positive feelings; and if the recipient eventually finds out who did the good deeds, so much the better.

3. *Concentrate on giving rather than on receiving.* Make this the emphasis at Christmastime. As you help each child with his shopping, help him to contemplate how good family members will feel when they receive his gifts. If possible, let your children make gifts for each other rather than merely buy them, thus putting more of themselves into the gift giving.

4. *Participate in family projects that help those in need.* Do painting or yard work for an elderly neighbor. Shovel snow off of the neighbors' sidewalks; if possible, keeping who did it a secret. Go as a family to the Church welfare farm or cannery and then talk to your family afterward about how the great Church welfare program helps those in need. Make these activities fun, and sometimes go out for a treat after the work has been done.

5. *Be a living example of service for your children.* One of the authors recalls the following experience:

When I was a boy, our stake owned a welfare farm, and the crop that was produced was sugar beets. City boy though I was, I became well acquainted with the processes of thinning, weeding, and topping beets. Whenever the call came to go to the welfare farm, my father volunteered our services. Sometimes there were very few others there, and my father and I were always among the very last to leave. I learned the lesson that no matter how long the row, you never stop in the middle. How grateful I was to see dad finish his rows and then double back to help me finish mine! I must confess that my father's diligence irritated me at times. Some able-bodied men and boys never came to the welfare farm; others felt that if they put in an hour's worth of work their duty was done. It didn't seem fair that we did so much more work than most of the members of the ward. Now, as I look back at those times, I really appreciate the lessons my father taught me—attention to duty, persistence, and lack of concern for what others did or didn't do.

What kind of example of service do you present to your children? When ward members are in the hospital, do you visit them? How long has it been since you went to see that elderly man or woman in your neighborhood who is confined to bed or to a wheelchair? In priesthood meeting or Relief Society when the call for a welfare or service project comes, is yours one of the first hands to be raised, or do you sit with lowered eyes hoping that enough others will volunteer so that the assignment will be filled without you? After a snowstorm do you hurry to shovel off the walk of the elderly widow a few houses away, or do you wait, hoping that another neighbor will get there first? Are you always prepared with ready-made excuses, or are you willing to set aside your personal plans when the call for service comes? Remember, the example you set for your child is the greatest single determinant as to whether or not he learns to find joy in serving others.

Summary

In this chapter we have suggested that there is a close relationship between the value a person places on others and the value he places on himself. A child who continually looks for and finds the worst in other people does not usually hold himself in high esteem. We can help children learn to look for the good in others; and a number of ways of doing this are outlined and discussed.

We love those whom we serve. We need to help our children find joy in serving others. The example of service that we model for our children is all-important. Family projects which help the needy can also help our children to find joy in serving others. Teach your children to do good anonymously for others, with no expectation of thanks or reward. Encourage them to come to you with *good* reports of what others have done; minimize and discourage bad reports.

As our children learn to look for the good in others and to gain practice in serving others, their feelings of confidence and self-esteem will grow.

Help Your Child to Give Love and Receive Love

6

"Beloved, let us love one another: for love is of God; and every one that loveth is born of God, and knoweth God. He that loveth not knoweth not God; for God is love."
(1 John 4:7-8.)

There is a story of an old Scot who lost his wife after forty years of marriage. A friend who came to console him remarked about the many virtues of the deceased, to which the husband replied: "Aye! She was a wonderful woman. And I came mighty close to telling her so once or twice."

There are many people who find it difficult to compliment their mate or to say those three simple little words, "I love you." Yet those words, sincerely stated, probably have more power to encourage, to motivate, and to bless lives than any other phrase in the English language. How sad it is that embarrassment or false pride or stubbornness are sometimes allowed to interfere with an expression of love. In a successful marriage words, such as "I love you" and tender acts which prove that love should be daily occurrences.

Just as some find it hard to communicate expressions of love to spouses, some find it difficult to show love for their children. To say "I love you" may be too embarrassing; or they may worry about how the child would react to such an expression. A well-known public-service commercial sponsored by the Church says, "If you love 'em, tell 'em—a thought from The Church of Jesus Christ of Latter-day Saints (the Mormons)."

Teach Your Child Love by Example

It has been said that the greatest gift a man can give to his children is the knowledge that he loves their mother. Some parents are reluctant to show any affection toward each other while the children are around. This is a mistake. It is good for children to hear parents express love for each other, and to see them hold hands, put their arms around each other, and kiss each other. The knowledge that parents love each other gives a child a secure feeling that he also is loved. It also provides a model for him later in openly expressing love for others.

When there are serious parental conflicts or divorce in a home, there may be devastating effects upon the child's feelings of lovability and self-esteem. In cases where divorce is imminent, or where parents have stopped loving each other, it is important to reassure the child that this has nothing to do with their feelings for him. Sometimes a parent who has been hurt tries to tear down the image of the other parent, or tell the child that the other parent doesn't love him anymore. This attempt to get back at the spouse is unwise and cruel. If the child accepts this statement as fact, there may be very adverse effects upon his self-concept. For the child's sake, parents should speak well of each other and protect one another's image, even when disaffection has occurred.

Effects of Love Deprivation

Children who do not receive enough love in their early years sometimes develop a condition called "affect hunger." They have an insatiable need for love, but often find it hard to accept the fact that they are loved, even when they are. Sometimes this leads to promiscuity—the need for a new relationship, a new conquest—in order to prove to themselves that they are really lovable. And yet they never feel really loved. A girl who does not feel that she is lovable is likely to sell herself very cheaply. She has low self-esteem and may feel that the only way she can be accepted by boys is by allowing sexual favors. But her promiscuity leads to feelings of guilt that lead to feelings of even less self-worth. People who hold themselves in high regard do not need to compromise their standards and values in a desperate need to be loved.

Do Not Control Your Child's Behavior by Withholding Love

Mrs. Cramer has found that when five-year-old Terri misbehaves, a very effective way to correct her is to make a statement, such as "Mommy doesn't love little girls who act that way." Though effective on the surface, the technique is not a good one to use. Not to be loved poses a real threat to most children, and they may be willing to do almost anything to keep love from being withdrawn. But, though behavior may temporarily improve, the child's feelings of confidence and lovability tend to erode and his self-esteem diminishes.

There is a temptation to say to our children, in word or action, "I love you when you do the things I tell you to do; I don't love you when you misbehave." You should not succumb to that temptation. Your child should know that parental love is not something that waxes and wanes. It is always there like the mountain to the east or the air that he breathes. Try to separate the child himself from his actions, and when he misbehaves let him know that it is the *behavior* that you dislike, not him personally.

A parent who controls the child's behavior by withholding love runs the risk that the child may learn that two can play the same game. As he gets older he may attempt to manipulate the parents by giving or withholding love himself.

Love Your Child for Himself—Not for His Accomplishments

Gary, age fourteen, is a Star Scout. He has not taken to Scouting like his older brother, Carl, who was an Eagle Scout before his fourteenth birthday. Gary feels bad about "letting his parents down," so he continues to plug away halfheartedly on merit badges. His older brother is also an accomplished musician and plays in the school orchestra and frequently at Church meetings. Gary has only average musical abilities. Though the parents have never made statements comparing him negatively with Carl, Gary sees himself as "dumb" and is convinced that his parents love Carl much more than they love him.

The two main ingredients of self-esteem are feelings of lovability and feelings of capability. But it is important that they be maintained separately, not intermixed. It would be unfortunate for your child to feel that he is lovable only if he is capable. He needs to feel cherished just because he is the unique person that he is, apart from whatever capabilities he has or does not have.

Display Physical Affection Toward Your Children

In some families brothers and sisters freely embrace and kiss each other; while in other families, though there is equal affection, outward displays of affection are restrained. If you were raised in the first kind of home, you have an advantage in that hugging and kissing your own children will come naturally. If your childhood was spent in the second kind of home, you may have to work a bit harder at displaying affection. Appropriate physical displays of affection in your home can contribute greatly to your children's feelings of being loved.

It is obvious that displays of affection among family members must be sincere and heartfelt. False displays of affection are easy to detect and are distasteful to children. Such phoniness causes a child to feel manipulated rather than loved, and it lowers his self-esteem rather than raises it.

Tell Them You Love Them

Some people suppose that their acts of support, duty, and kindness are sufficient indications of their love, while their spouses long to hear those "three magic words." We need to express our feelings of love vocally to our husbands or wives. Our children also need to hear us say we love them, and they need to know we are absolutely sincere when we say it. If you have a teenager in your home, think for a minute—how long has it been since you verbalized your love for him or her? Don't let another day go by—tell him today! If you feel embarrassed, or are afraid you will embarrass the child, then practice saying it a few times to yourself and then at an opportune moment gather up all your courage and try it out. Realize that if you haven't made a practice of saying "I love you," you may thoroughly confuse your teenager at first. He may even think you are being sarcastic or trying to manipulate him. But once he realizes that you have no ulterior motive and are completely sincere, you may be amazed at the changes that take place in his behavior and self-concept.

Teach Your Child to Love Our Father in Heaven and Jesus

A first and very important step in learning to love God is to learn to love his children. John expressed the thought this way: "If a man say, I love God, and hateth his brother, he is a liar: for he that loveth not his brother whom he hath seen, how can he love God whom he hath not seen?" (1 John 4:20.) Christ said to his followers, "A new commandment I give unto you, That ye love one another; as I have loved you, that ye also love one another" (John 13:34). The little song that our children sing in Primary says:

> Jesus said love everyone,
> Treat them kindly too,
> When your heart is filled with love
> Others will love you.
> ("Jesus Said Love Everyone" *Sing With Me*, B-51.)

Jesus made it clear that it is easy to love those who love us—even the heathens and the publicans do that. He expects his followers to love everyone—even their enemies. Certainly to teach our children to dislike others merely because they are of a different political party, religion, or skin color is contrary to the wishes of our Father in Heaven. All mankind are our brothers and sisters, and God loves all of his children.

How can we best teach our children to love God? First and foremost, by exemplifying that love ourselves. In our conduct and leadership in the home, in the way we live God's commandments, and in the way we address our Father in Heaven in prayer we demonstrate our faith in and love for God. One child said, "When my father gives the family prayer or the blessing on the food I almost have to open my eyes to see if the Lord is standing right there, because it seems like he is really talking to him." Wouldn't it be wonderful if all children could have this kind of experience as they listen to prayers that are offered in their homes? We need to teach our children to put their trust in God and to know that he is a loving Father who knows them and their needs and wants them to have success and joy. What a boost to our children's self-esteem!

Summary

Nothing will have as much positive effect upon your child's self-esteem as his feeling of being really loved. Our children need to feel loved for themselves, not for what they can accomplish. Parents should not control their children's behavior by withholding love. Tell your children frequently that you love them and reinforce this love by your actions and by appropriate displays of affection. Teach them to love other people, and then use this love as a springboard to learning to love God. Teach them by your own example to love God and trust in him. If you can increase your children's feelings of being sincerely loved, you will add immeasurably to their feelings of self-worth.

Treat Your Child With Courtesy and Consideration

7

"No power or influence can or ought to be maintained by virtue of the priesthood, only by persuasion, by long-suffering, by gentleness and meekness, and by love unfeigned; by kindness and pure knowledge, which shall greatly enlarge the soul without hypocrisy, and without guile"
(D&C 121:41-42).

Sometimes we think of our children as literally "our children," in the same sense as "our home" or "our car." When we think a little more carefully, of course, we realize that in that sense they are not our children at all. We may say that they belong to themselves and to our Father in Heaven. They are entrusted to our care for a few years to rear them to maturity. Their spirits are probably as old as ours, even though we arrived here twenty plus years earlier than they, we to become the parents and they the children.

Some adults seem to think that, though children are always to show proper respect to adults, parents can treat them in any way they wish. Children do need adult direction, and parents need to exercise adult control and leadership. But this can be done in ways that show respect for children and that help them maintain self-esteem. There are some areas in which children need to be treated as equals.

Teach Your Child to Show Courtesy and Consideration for Others

How can we best teach our children to exercise proper respect for adults and to use good manners? Treating them with respect and using good manners when dealing with them are the most effective ways. Can we expect children in a family to treat each other with consideration and courtesy if parents do not model these traits themselves? If we find it necessary to walk in front of a child, we should say "Excuse me," just as readily as if it were another adult. We should say "Please" when we ask a child to do something for us and "Thank you" after it has been done, just as if it were a neighbor or friend. Good manners are artificial and foreign to a child who has not grown up with them; they come as natural as breathing to a child who has experienced them in the home.

Avoid Negative or Demeaning Approaches

Nagging and scolding are among the negative responses many parents make. They are remarkably ineffective ways of bringing about improved behavior in children. They cause resentment and antagonism as well as diminish children's self-esteem. When constant nagging occurs, in order to protect feelings of self-worth children may stop listening and become "psychologically deaf." Parents should learn to approach children in a more positive fashion.

Along with nagging and scolding, sarcasm and ridicule can have devastating effects on the child's self-esteem. Consider such statements as these:

"How stupid! I've told you a thousand times to change your church clothes as soon as you get home. I don't think I can ever get those pants clean again."

"Hazel, if you keep eating so much candy and so many desserts, you're going to have even more trouble getting into your clothes than you do now!"

"Mark, I told you before to knock off that foolishness. Why must you always make such a sap out of yourself?"

"Well, listen to little Mr. Know-it-all! Why, you must be the smartest kid in the whole world."

Or how about comments made to other people about the child, in the child's presence?

"What am I going to do with this child? The little brat won't do a thing I say!"

"My Sally is so shy! Look how she blushes when I talk about her."

"Max never listens to a thing I tell him; his head's always in the clouds."

"For two cents I'd give this kid back to the Indians."

Obviously, comments such as these are ill-advised and can damage a child's self-esteem.

Treat Children Like People, and Teach Them to Interact Appropriately With Adults

A generation ago it was common to hear the statement "Children should be seen and not heard." Today the opposite is often true; children are allowed to dominate the scene and to keep adults from carrying on a sustained conversation. Neither of these extremes is satisfactory. If children are taught to mingle with adults in appropriate ways, they can learn social skills and become comfortable with people.

In a group situation involving both children and adults, the children should be treated as people—not just ignored. Consider this situation: Bill and Art go on a fishing trip, and Bill takes his ten-year-old son, Bob. Most of the time the men talk about adult topics and pay little attention to Bob. They never draw him into the conversation or talk about anything that is of interest to him. Bill and Art would never treat another adult this way, and if they did they would offend him with such rudeness.

Contrast this situation with another incident which one of the authors observed in a restaurant. A middle-aged man and woman were at lunch with their grandson, who was five or six years of age. During the entire time all conversation was addressed to the child: "Tommy, isn't this fun?" "Tommy, where did you get that nice shirt?" "Tommy, what is Santa Claus going to bring you for Christmas?" "Tommy, look at that funny big dog outside!" Not once were grandpa and grandma heard to address each other; they kept the boy in the spotlight with a constant stream of conversation. He probably would have enjoyed himself more if they had left him alone part of the time.

Somewhere between the two men who ignored the child when on a fishing trip and the doting grandparents at the restaurant there is a happy medium. A child should be treated as a valued and respected member of the group—not as a non-entity or as the center of the universe.

Try Not to Embarrass Your Child

Think back to the last time you were embarrassed. Was it because of something that someone said or did? How did it make you feel? Embarrassment happens to everyone, of course, but as much as possible parents should avoid bringing it about.

A very poor time to correct your child is when other people are around, especially the child's friends. Consider these examples:

"Curtis, I wish you wouldn't always look so slouchy when you pass the sacrament; I noticed today how much neater Steven looked than you. Straighten up next time and keep your shirttail tucked in."

"Carrie, I'll bet your mother would about die if your room looked as bad as Linda's."

"George, must you always and forever show off? I'll bet your friends think you're an idiot."

"Susan, I'm surprised at your report card—three C's, two B's, and only one A. Anna, let me see your report card. I'll bet you did a lot better!"

"Henry, you get back in here! How come you're so stupid? Don't you know enough to put a coat on? Look at Frank, he's got his coat on."

Comments like these would be bad enough even if no one else were around, but to shame a child in front of others is doubly bad. Such action causes hostile feelings and adversely affects self-esteem. Certainly a parent should use more positive and tactful methods of interaction with children.

Help Your Child to Save Face

We all make mistakes, and how grateful we are when a friend pretends not to notice or diverts attention to something else to cover up the mistake! The last thing we need is for our "friend" to laugh rudely at the mistake, or to bring it up again and again, or to amuse his friends at our expense. This also is the last thing our child needs us to do.

A wise teacher (or parent) on occasion covers up for a child's ridiculous question or comment with statements like: "Oh, I see why Terry thought that was so. Because...." "That's an easy mistake to make." "That's an interesting question. Let's talk about it later." The teacher is sometimes able to twist an entirely irrelevant comment in order for it to bear some relationship to the discussion. With these techniques the teacher can avoid embarrassing the child and thereby protect his feelings of self-worth. You can learn to use some of these same approaches. By all means avoid tactics of one-upmanship. Don't feel the need to prove your child wrong even when he is.

Be Sure That the Demands You Make Are Reasonable

Brother Oldham told his high priests group leader, Brother Saunders, that his junior companion is never available to go with him to visit their families and asked that he be allowed to have his wife go with him instead. The truth of the matter is that Brother Oldham never makes plans or checks with the boy ahead of time. He never asks him what the most convenient time is for him. His usual practice is to call the boy ten minutes before he plans to go out, only to find him away from home or in the middle of something he cannot just suddenly drop. If Brother Oldham's companion were an adult, a member of his quorum, he would not treat him in this fashion.

It is easy for adults to think that their time is more important than a child's time, their plans more important than a child's plans, their activities more important than a child's activities. This attitude is not fair to young people. While parents should not make themselves slaves to their children and cater to their every whim, neither should they expect their children to be slaves to them. Children deserve the same consideration that we would give to adults.

Summary

This chapter mentions ways in which parents can enhance self-esteem by treating children with courtesy and consideration. You should model for your children the courtesy and consideration that you want them to display. Avoid the use of ridicule and sarcasm, nagging and scolding. Use positive methods whenever you can. Teach your children to interact with adults in appropriate ways. Protect your children against unnecessary embarrassment; and when you have to correct them, do it in private. Make sure that your demands are reasonable. Perhaps it could be best summed up by saying that you should treat your children like *persons,* not like possessions. Treat them the way you treat your best friends, and perhaps they will think of you as their best friends.

Care Enough to Discipline Your Child

8

*"For whom the Lord loveth he
correcteth; even as a father the son in
whom he delighteth"*
(Proverbs 3:12).

Jana is fourteen years old. Since her family lives in an area that is not predominantly LDS, most of her friends are not members of the Church. Jana is attractive and has constant opportunities for dates. She wants to be like her friends and is embarrassed to tell them, and the boys who ask her, that her parents consider her too young to date.

Jana's parents want to follow the counsel of Church leaders and postpone Jana's dating until she reaches sixteen. On the other hand, they want her to be popular with and accepted by her friends. They are tempted to consider their situation a special case because Jana is more mature than the average girl her age and because dating is approved by her friends and their parents.

Though Jana is continually pushing to get her parents to change their minds, she herself has mixed feelings about accepting social invitations from boys. She generally trusts and follows the counsel of Church leaders and is not sure that she is justified in doing otherwise in this case. Furthermore, she is not sure she wants to be paired off with a single boy, though she enjoys being in social situations where both boys and girls are present. In a very real sense Jana's parents, while ostensibly restricting her against her wishes, are really providing security for her; she can say, "My parents won't allow me to date until I'm sixteen," and put the pressure on them rather than on herself. It is very likely that if her parents do give in, she will lose some respect for them for not being stronger and holding to their own principles and for not providing the security and protection she secretly appreciates. Their willingness to set limits and impose sanctions tells Jana that they really care for her.

What would be a wiser course of action for Jana's parents than succumbing to the pressures to allow dating? They should provide frequent opportunities for social interaction in mixed groups, both formal and informal. They should make their home a place where young people of both sexes feel welcome and at ease. They should have boy-girl parties and allow Jana to plan the activities and the refreshments. If Jana's home gets the reputation of a fun place to be, the fact that she has to wait a little while to date is likely to be relatively unimportant.

The True Meaning of Discipline

Discipline comes from the same root as *disciple*. A disciple is a follower; and discipline is best described as a system of leadership rather than of punishment. Early in life the child follows the parents, often quite blindly, since he is not intellectually mature enough to understand all of the reasons. As the child gets older, parental discipline gradually gives way to self-discipline in which the child learns to follow principles and ideals which have been internalized.

To many people, *discipline* is synonymous with *punishment*. But punishment is only one aspect of discipline, and not one of the best aspects at that. The old adage "You can catch more flies with honey than with vinegar" certainly applies to raising children. Positive incentives generate good feelings toward those who provide the rewards; punishment often causes bad feelings toward the punishing adult rather than a hatred of the behavior that brought on the punishment. Furthermore, the punished child is apt to feel guilty or inferior, whereas the rewarded child receives a psychological boost to self-esteem.

If you are like most parents, you will not be able to avoid punishment altogether, desirable as that would be. It is hard to find a positive approach to some behaviors. In this dispensation the Lord has said, "Reproving betimes with sharpness, when moved upon by the Holy Ghost; and then showing forth afterwards an increase of love toward him whom thou hast reproved, lest he esteem thee to be his enemy" (D&C 121:43). This is excellent advice for parents; after all, what better source could we ask for?

The phrase "when moved upon by the Holy Ghost" is a key one. Whatever we do under the influence of the Holy Ghost will be a correct action. If we live in accordance with the principles of the gospel and then devoutly seek the Lord's assistance and advice, how can we go wrong? If we punish a child under these conditions, the punishment will be mild, our motivation being the child's welfare. But if we punish out of vindictiveness and anger, the punishment may be overly severe, our motivation being the release of our own tensions and hostile feelings.

When Possible, Use Natural and Logical Consequences Instead of Punishment

Though you need not feel guilty if you resort to mild punishment on occasion, when you are able to use rewards or help your children see that good behavior brings about good consequences, you will see more positive results in behavior and in self-esteem. Punishment is often arbitrary and not related to the behavior that occasioned it. With the use of natural or logical consequences the outcome is not arbitrary, and the child is more likely to associate it with his own behavior rather than to blame his misfortune on his parents. Furthermore, instead of becoming angry and antagonizing the child, with the use of natural consequences the parent can remain calm and sympathetic.

First of all, let's distinguish between a natural consequence and a logical consequence. A natural consequence is something that naturally occurs as a result of one's action; a logical consequence is externally imposed, but there is a logical connection between the action and the result. Natural and logical consequences can, of course, be either positive or negative in nature.

Let's illustrate with some examples: Mr. Rollins has told his son Brad that if he doesn't complete the requirements for his Star Scout advancement by a certain date he will get no more allowance until he does. How can Brad's father shift over to the use of consequences instead of punishment in encouraging achievement in Scouting?

First of all, can he leave it just to natural consequences? What are the natural consequences of Brad's not attaining the Star rank? If Brad has friends in the troop who are moving ahead, Brad may be motivated to do the same to avoid the embarrassment of falling behind. The anticipated positive consequences of attaining a new rank would include the recognition from family and friends, praise from the Scoutmaster, and the addition of one more decoration on the Scout uniform. It could even be that the threat of punishment Brad's father is imposing is having a reverse effect, and that if he would just ease off a bit, Brad would move ahead faster.

But what if the natural consequences do not appear to be strong enough to provide motivation? Then the father might look for a logical consequence. A good Scoutmaster might already be applying some logical consequences. If an important trip is planned several months in advance, he may stipulate that only the boys who make a rank advancement or earn a certain number of merit badges can go on the trip. The logic of this consequence might be explained that through their advancements they demonstrate their maturity and their interest in Scouting, or even that the skills developed in the advancement will be needed on the trip. If, in spite of encouragement and assistance from the father, the Scoutmaster, and others, Brad fails to achieve, there is no need for the father to become angry. The loss of the trip is consequence enough. In this case parents can sympathize with him and say, "We're sure sorry you have to stay home," and this can be a

very truthful statement, free of rancor, thus precluding any
negative effects on the parent-child relationship.

Here are some other examples of the use of natural and
logical consequences rather than punishment:

Punishment	Natural or Logical Consequence
"Since you didn't clean up your room, you can't go to the movie."	"I was going to make banana-cream pie for dessert. But I couldn't stand the sight of your room any longer, so I spent my time cleaning your room instead. I'm sorry, I know that's your favorite dessert."
"I've told you time and again to let me know where you're going. I'm going to have to ground you until next Tuesday."	"Bob came over to see you an hour ago. He was able to get tickets for the concert after all. I couldn't tell him where to find you, so he took Cindy instead."
"You're altogether too forgetful. When you forgot your lunch this morning, I had to run it over to you and I wasted a whole hour of my time. To teach you a lesson you'll have to work an hour in the garden."	"Sorry you missed lunch today. I put it in the fridge, and you can take it tomorrow."
"Wake up! Wake up! If it weren't for me I doubt you'd ever make it to that first-period class."	"Hope you didn't miss too much by sleeping through your first-period class again."

Too often parents pity children and protect them too much
from the natural consequences of their behavior. If we become

slaves to our children and are always there to protect them from themselves, we make them dependent. Obviously we cannot let a child suffer the consequence of his behavior in a dangerous or life-threatening situation. But if he suffers some less serious consequence, he will learn a lesson and behave differently next time. If your child has to stand on his own two feet and be responsible for his own behavior, he becomes a more independent and responsible person and his feelings of capability and self-esteem are enhanced.

Avoid Permissiveness and Be Willing to Discipline

Tom is the envy of his fifteen-year-old "jet set." While his friends have to be home at a set time, Tom can cavort around all night if he wishes. His parents leave the door unlocked for him, and then they go to bed and to sleep, seldom knowing (or caring?) what time he arrives home. They make few demands upon him and seldom know where he is, who he is with, or what he is doing. Though Tom boasts of his freedom, secretly he envies children whose parents impose reasonable limits.

Why might parents fail to provide the discipline that a child needs? They may fear that if they are too strict they will lose the child's love. They may worry about the child, but not know how to cope with the behavior or they may not know what approach to try and so do nothing. Or they may be too busy with their own affairs to even know what the child is doing. But, whatever the reason, the child is apt to interpret a lack of discipline as a lack of caring. He asks himself, "Why don't my parents make me do the things I should be doing?" Sometimes a child like this will continually "test the limits" by making his behavior progressively more objectionable, unconsciously saying, "Just how far do I have to go before somebody stops me?" The worse his behavior, the more likely the feelings of guilt and worthlessness. The misbehaving child is almost always a child with low self-esteem.

Summary

The best discipline is not punishment, but effective leadership. Whenever possible you should use a positive approach instead of punishment to correct your child's behavior. Even better than either praise or punishment is the use of natural or logical consequences. Poor methods of discipline work against self-esteem, while good methods enhance it. When parents neglect discipline, children increase misbehavior and "test the limits." They seek some evidence that the parent cares about them enough to be concerned about what they do. Low self-esteem causes misbehavior, and misbehavior in turn causes feelings of guilt, worthlessness, and low self-esteem.

Spend Quality Time With Your Child

9

"But Jesus said, Suffer little children, and forbid them not, to come unto me: for of such is the kingdom of heaven"
(Matthew 19:14).

The scriptures report that little children were brought to Jesus that he might bless them. His disciples rebuked those who brought them, possibly feeling that the Master was too tired or too busy with weightier matters to bother with mere children. It was at this time that Jesus commanded them to let the little children come to him. He loved children and wanted to grant the blessings that the parents desired for their children. So he was willing to set aside the fatigue he felt or the matters that others may have felt were more important.

Are there times when your children seek your time and attention at very awkward moments—just when you're finally getting around to some duty you've been procrastinating for lack of time, or just when you are so worn-out from hard work that all you want to do is crawl into the tub and soak your weary bones and relax? Unfortunately, we cannot always plan carefully and choose the time that is best for us—events happen spontaneously and unexpectedly. And when the child needs us, it may be at that very moment, not an hour or two later. A mature adult is able, at times, to set aside his own needs in order to make time for his children.

Make Time With Your Children a High Priority

Mr. Carlson is an important executive in a large corporation. He finds that he must spend at least sixty hours a week on the job in order to meet his company's expectations.

Mr. Hansen is heavily involved in athletics throughout the entire year. During the winter season, when he is not actively involved in basketball or bowling, he spends evenings refereeing local basketball contests. Whenever the weather permits in spring or summer, he is on the golf course; and he plays in a foursome every Sunday morning.

Bishop Martin wears his mantle very heavily. There are many young couples in his ward, and they are pleased to find that the bishop is concerned for their welfare. In his employment he is a professional counselor, and he is sure that the Lord called him to his Church position, at least in part, because of his expertise in helping people to resolve their personal problems. He spends several evenings a week in counseling, in addition to the regular duties his office includes.

What do Mr. Carlson, Mr. Hansen, and Bishop Martin have in common? They are all so busy that their own children see very little of them. Their wives shoulder most of the burden of child rearing. Seldom are they able to attend piano recitals, school programs, or other events that involve their children. Family recreational activities almost always take place without them. Often they arrive home after the children are in bed. What a big price these men are paying! Their children hardly know them, and they hardly know their children. How can they hope to be very important influences in their children's lives?

An oft-quoted statement of President David O. McKay is, "No other success can compensate for failure in the home." A similar sentiment was expressed by President Harold B. Lee when he said, "The greatest of the Lord's work you will ever do as fathers will be within the walls of your own home." Our families must not take second place even to Church work if we are to exert the positive influence in our children's lives that will help them develop self-esteem.

Sometimes a parent will feel guilty about the little time he spends with a child and will attempt to compensate by buying the child elaborate or expensive gifts. Though this may salve the parent's conscience, it is quite ineffective in building a relationship. The only gift that ultimately makes much difference is the gift of self.

Treat Your Children As Individuals

Not only does good parenting require a sacrifice of parents' time, but that time must also be given on an individual basis. Periodically gathering the children as a group around you is not enough. Ideally, each child in a family should have some individual time every day with each parent. This time may be difficult to arrange, especially in a large family, but the desirable benefits are worth the effort.

An insightful parent knows that each child must be treated differently, because everyone is different and responds to different motivations. If a father takes his three sons with him on a fishing trip, one or more of them may be fascinated by the opportunity and the others may be thoroughly bored. You need to be with your children enough to know their individual personalities and preferences, and then use this knowledge in deciding how best to relate to each child.

Involve Your Child in Your Own Activities When Appropriate

You may feel that your time is already allocated to the essentials of living and wonder how you can squeeze out any more time for individual children. But it is not always necessary to create *extra* time; you can sometimes involve your children in activities that you would be doing anyway. Small children love to accompany a parent on errands, such as going to the store or to the bank. Instead of listening to the radio or daydreaming, you can involve the child in conversation. It is a fine opportunity to get to know the child better and see what thoughts occupy his attention. It also gives your child a chance to get better acquainted with you. Young children also like to help, and allowing them to do so can be the first step in helping them to feel capable and in teaching them to enjoy work.

As your children get a little older, going to the store or helping mom or dad will both lose some appeal. Then you have to find other ways to involve them. If you have enjoyed fishing, hunting, ball games, shopping trips, fashion shows, or other activities, now may be the time to invite your children to participate with you.

Quality Versus Quantity

A father who is at home almost every night may pride himself on the fact that he is spending time with his family; but if most of that time is spent with his face in the newspaper or in front of the television set, with very little interaction with his wife or children, he might just as well be away. A mother may be so busy bustling about the home, taking care of daily chores, doing sewing or quilting projects, baking, canning, preparing her Primary lesson, or carrying out a self-improvement project, that there is not much time left to spend with her family. Her children might get the impression that the mother sees these activities as more important than time spent with them.

The quality of the time spent with your child is much more important than the amount of time spent. Watching television, movies, or spectator sports together provides little opportunity for interaction and is relatively unproductive in building a relationship. But activities, such as fishing, hunting, camping, shopping, playing ball, or simply sitting and talking, allow for significant interactions to take place.

Be sure that a lot of the time you spend with your children is mutually enjoyable. If you spend the time grudgingly, with one eye on your watch, your children will sense that you are with them only out of a sense of duty, and the experience is less likely to build self-esteem. A willing gift of your time says to your child: "Dad and Mom like to be with me. They think I'm okay." As your child feels lovable and wanted, his feelings of self-worth are enhanced.

Spend Quiet Time With Your Child at Bedtime

Jason had an aversion to going to bed. It didn't seem fair for him to have to go to bed at 8:00 P.M., while his older brother and sister stayed up much later. It was especially galling to hear the sound of the popcorn popper, followed by the aroma of melted butter, or to hear the happy sounds of family members playing a game together. He usually didn't feel tired at eight o'clock, and besides, though he didn't like to admit it, he didn't really feel comfortable in that dark room all alone.

Once Jason's parents understood his feelings and the reasons for his resistance to bed, the solution was easy. Mom and dad began to take turns spending just ten or fifteen minutes with him after he was in bed. Sometimes there was a story, or a game, or a quiet song. Sometimes they just discussed the events of the day. The parents also decided that if there were games to be played or refreshments to be enjoyed, they would do it early enough for Jason to be involved or wait until after he had fallen asleep. Jason began to look forward to bedtime rather than to dread it, and would often ask the parents, "Which one is going to come in and talk to me tonight?"

Bedtime is a good time to give your child emotional support, a little psychological boost. This can be a happy time that your child can look forward to, a peaceful time to wind down from a busy and perhaps hectic day.

Help Your Child Learn to Share You With Others

A child who enjoys individual time with parents should be willing to allow the same consideration for his brothers and sisters. You and your spouse also need to plan your time so that you have ample time to spend with each other. It is not uncommon for parents to subjugate their own needs to those of their children to such an extent that their relationship to each other suffers. It may become painfully clear to the husband and wife after the last child leaves the "nest" that they have centered their lives so much around their children and have tried so hard to meet the children's needs, that they have forgotten how to relate to each other.

If yours happens to be a home in which there is a handicapped child, you need to take care to see that your nonhandicapped children do not feel that all of your time, attention, and even love are expended toward the child who needs special help. You should teach your children at a very early age to perform some of the needed service for the handicapped child so that you will have the time to give attention to other family members. The old saying "Whom we serve, we love" is true. By helping to take care of the needs of the less fortunate child, your "normal" children can further their own feelings of competence, love, and self-esteem.

Make Family Time Quality Time

Probably in no other dispensation of time has the importance of the family been stressed as much as in this one, the dispensation of the fulness of times. Satan knows that his time is short. He also knows that few efforts on his part will accomplish as much for him and do as much to frustrate God's eternal plan as to disrupt family life and to sow seeds of discord among family members. The challenge for LDS parents is great. But one real advantage we have is in the quality of our children. We are told that the Lord has reserved some of the most choice spirits to come forth in this dispensation. Parents have no greater calling than to promote family solidarity and harmonious relationships in the home.

Parents who neglect family prayer, family home evening, and other quality family activities do so at their own peril and at the expense of their children. Quality time spent with all family members together helps to build family pride and family solidarity. The love and support of family members can really enhance a child's self-esteem.

The consolidated meeting schedule in which almost all Church meetings take place in a three-hour block on Sunday has opened the way for us to spend more time with our children. A family lesson and other Sunday-type family activities can take place on Sundays. The Monday family home evening in which families often alternate lessons and activities can include educational, cultural, and recreational activities which involve the whole family. A wise LDS parent will give high priority to a family lesson on Sunday and either a lesson or a family activity on Monday night. Quality time spent with all family members together helps to build family pride and to foster feelings of security among family members.

Summary

A mature parent is able to set aside his own needs at times in order to make time for his children. Parents who let employment, recreational activities, or even Church work interfere with good relationships with their children pay too heavy a price. Expensive gifts will not compensate for lack of time spent with the child. The quality of time that parents spend with children is much more important than the mere quantity. Bedtime often affords a good time for parents to have a quiet time with their children. Family solidarity is promoted by family members working together, having fun together, praying and reading scriptures together, and carrying out family traditions. And family solidarity and a willing gift of parental time help children to develop feelings of lovability, capability, and self-esteem.

Let Your Child Make His Own Decisions

10

"For behold, it is not meet that I should command in all things; for he that is compelled in all things, the same is a slothful and not a wise servant.... Verily I say, men should be anxiously engaged in a good cause, and do many things of their own free will."
(D&C 58:26-27.)

Shirley just graduated from high school and will be starting college in the fall. She wants to buy some new clothes for school. Because she has had a part-time job for two years, she is able to finance most of the cost of her new wardrobe herself. Shirley would like to go with her friends to shop for the clothes, but her mother feels that because so much money is involved she should personally help Shirley decide which clothes to buy. She is so persuasive that Shirley ends up buying mostly clothes that her mother likes and feels are appropriate.

Is mother right in involving herself so actively in clothes selection for Shirley? There would be nothing wrong with her going to the store with her daughter or offering suggestions when solicited. But for the mother to take the prime role in deciding which clothes to purchase may be wrong, especially since Shirley's earnings are paying for most of the purchases. By the end of high school a child should be able to decide pretty much what clothes to buy. If Shirley is a normal young lady, she may resent her mother's inflicting choices upon her. Some of the clothes are likely to hang in the closet for weeks or months at a time, unloved and unworn.

Too often parents feel they can keep children from making any mistakes by making decisions for them. But even if this were true, would it be a good thing to do? Though mistakes are annoying, inconvenient, and sometimes costly, they provide an opportunity to learn from experience and to make better choices next time.

Make Only Those Choices for Your Child That Are Yours to Make

At any age there are choices the parent must make and others the child should be allowed to make. How can you know which are which? The guiding principle is that your child should not be allowed to make any decision in which a wrong choice involves an element of danger or harm to the child or to others. For example, your four-year-old cannot decide for himself whether he wants to play out in the busy street. Your teenaged daughter cannot decide to go off on an unchaperoned vacation with her boyfriend.

The older the child, the more important the decisions he is allowed to make. But in situations where a wrong choice may produce physical, moral, or psychological danger, the parent must make the final decision. A good question for you to ask is, "What difference will it make?" If there is a potential danger which would outweigh the advantage of the child's feelings of autonomy being promoted, then the parent must make the decision. If not, the decision should rest with the child.

It may be very painful for a mother to see her little girl go to school wearing a purple skirt, orange blouse, blue stockings, and red shoes. At another time a lesson in appropriate color combinations may certainly be in order. But if the mother asks herself, "What difference will it make?" she will probably decide that the mild ridicule her daughter may experience poses no real danger and may be a learning experience.

Let Your Child Make Decisions That Are Appropriate for His Age

At any age you can provide practice for your child in making decisions. A basic rule is that you should not allow your child to make any choices that you cannot live with. It is not wise to ask a young child questions, such as "Do you want to go to bed now?" or, "Do you want to come and eat now?" unless you really don't care whether he does it or not. The most natural and truthful response the child can make to questions of this kind is no. Parents too often ask such questions, and then when the child answers with a very predictable no they drag him protestingly to the table or to bed anyway. With a young child it is much better to simply pick him up and carry him to the bedroom or the table without asking him if he wants to go.

In the situation of dinner or bedtime it is possible to still present the child with alternatives, but only when you can live with either choice. You can ask, "Do you want to put your pajamas on here or in your bedroom?" or, "Do you want to ride piggyback or walk by yourself?" If you don't really care whether your child plays inside or out, you can give him a choice. But if you need a little breather—a time for yourself— don't say, "George, do you want to go outside and play?" Just help him on with his coat, say, "I want you to play outside for a while," and gently push him out of the door (assuming, of course, that there is adequate supervision, a protected area, or that the child is old enough to stay out of danger).

Shift Decisions Gradually From You to Your Child

Parents must learn to let go gradually. An infant has no power to make decisions for himself. But very early, even in the toddler stage, he needs to make decisions of a very simple nature. You should very gradually let the balance shift, with fewer decisions coming from you and more from your child, so that by late adolescence or early adulthood almost all decisions are his own.

If parents do not trust children to make appropriate decisions and decide for the child after he should be thinking for himself, two negative results are possible. The most likely one is that the child will become very dependent. He will not trust his own ideas and will always look to others for answers.

Eventually he may so distrust his ability to make decisions that he will accept almost anyone's judgment as superior to his own. The second possibility when parents insist on doing the child's thinking for him is that the child may become resentful and refuse to accept any advice from parents or other adults. He may do things behind the parents' backs that they would not approve of just to prove he is "his own person."

Teach Your Child Decision-making Skills

Instead of trying to make all of your children's decisions, you would do well to teach them decision-making skills. If you make a decision for a child, you may get him past an immediate situation; but if you teach him to make wise decisions for himself, you prepare him for life. The older your child becomes, the less knowledge you will have of his activities, and the less he will let you into his life.

There is no way we can be with our children twenty-four hours a day, benignly controlling their lives and keeping them from making mistakes. So our hope is that while they are young, dependent, and accepting of us as authority figures, we can teach them to think for themselves and learn to make their own decisions.

One way of teaching decision-making skills is to explore alternatives with your child, using questions and suggestions, such as "What would happen if...." "If she does that, what will you do?" "What are some ways you could handle that differently next time?" "How do you think that will make them feel?" "Let's write down some possible things you could do next time, and then decide which ways are best." As you use this technique, refrain from providing him with pat, ready-made solutions of your own. Let the ideas come from the child himself.

If you give your child practice in making small decisions along the way, you increase the chances that when he needs to make really important decisions later on in life, he will assert himself with confidence, have a feeling of capability, and arrive at wise decisions regarding his future.

Teach Your Child to Involve the Lord in His Decisions

If we teach our children while they are young to pray for the Lord's guidance, we increase the chances that they will continue to seek his advice in the important decisions they must make throughout life. The knowledge that a loving Father really listens and cares and that he will give us the inspiration we need will add immeasurably to the confidence we have in the decisions we make. Sometimes the help we need in making decisions comes to us through Church leaders whose calling it is to give counsel, and we need to teach our children to take advantage of the help that is available.

Important though it is to seek counsel from the Lord's servants and inspiration from him directly, it is equally important to realize that we should not expect either the Lord or our Church leaders to make our decisions for us. When Oliver Cowdery was given permission to attempt to translate some of the Book of Mormon writings and was unsuccessful, the Lord said to him:

> Behold, you have not understood; you have supposed that I would give it unto you, when you took no thought save it was to ask me.
> But, behold, I say unto you, that you must study it out in your mind; then you must ask me if it be right, and if it is right I will cause that your bosom shall burn within you; therefore, you shall feel that it is right.
> But if it be not right you shall have no such feelings, but you shall have a stupor of thought that shall cause you to forget the thing which is wrong. (D&C 9:7-9.)

Though the above passage pertains specifically to Oliver's attempt to translate, it could be applied to many other situations. We should teach our children that it is not appropriate to simply present the alternatives to God and expect him to tell us which to do. Rather we should weigh all alternatives and make the best decision we know how to make, and then ask the Lord in prayer if the decision be right. We need to teach our children to recognize the difference between the burning of the bosom within them and the stupor of thought spoken of by the Lord in the sciptures.

Teach Decision Making by Example

Your child has a much better chance of being a good decision-maker if you provide him with a good model rather than if you are wishy-washy and indecisive yourself. The basis of decision making in important situations is often the value system of the parent. If gospel principles form the basis of your value system, then certain decisions become automatic. As your child grows older he may reject some of your cherished values, but if you have made the values clear you have at least given him a starting point.

It is very painful for LDS parents to see their children reject the values they have been taught and perhaps even leave the Church. But often the rejection is only temporary—perhaps a reaction against parental pressures or a need for independence—and the children will return to parental values and to the Church later in life. It is sad when no clear-cut values have been taught and a child has nothing to return to, or to modify in terms of his own needs.

It is not too uncommon to hear a parent say something like this: "My parents pushed their religion down my throat. I'm not going to inflict my church upon my children. I'll let them learn about all churches, and then when they get old enough they can decide for themselves which church to join." An attitude such as this teaches children that religion is really not important, and there will probably be little motivation for a child in this kind of home to join any church.

Provide Practice in Decision Making by Giving Your Child an Allowance

One of the good things about giving a child an allowance is that it provides him with opportunities to choose how to spend the money. We suggest that the amount be moderate and be increased as the child gets older and be continued until he is old enough to earn his own money. Your child should have considerable freedom in deciding how to spend the money. It is quite appropriate for you to encourage him to set aside money for tithing and to insist that a certain other proportion be saved for a worthwhile purpose, such as a mission. But the

child can spend the rest in any way he wishes. It is painful to
see your child squander money, but not to let him make these
mistakes is to deny him a rich learning opportunity. It is far
better for him to learn by his mistakes while he is young and
the amount of money is small, than to foolishly spend larger
amounts of money later on. As he learns to spend his money
wisely, his feelings of capability increase and his self-esteem is
enhanced.

Provide Guidance for Your Children in Gospel Decisions

A parent asks, "Should I force my child to go to church?"
The answer to this question is not easy, and it may depend on
the situation and the age of the child. On principle we are
opposed to force. In the premortal life Satan's plan was to
force all of God's children to do good. The Father's plan was to
give them their free agency, even though it would obviously
mean that many would be lost along the way.

One of our hymns written by William C. Clegg and set to
music by Evan Stephens says:

> Know this, that every soul is free
> To choose his life and what he'll be;
> For this eternal truth is given,
> That God will force no man to heav'n.

> He'll call, persuade, direct aright
> And bless with wisdom, love, and light,
> In nameless ways be good and kind,
> But never force the human mind.

> ("Know This, That Every Soul Is Free,"
> *Hymns,* no. 90.)

God's way of dealing with us, his children, provides a perfect
example of how we should deal with our children. We cannot
force our children to live good lives and obey gospel principles. The Lord has told us to use persuasion, long-suffering,
gentleness, meekness, and love unfeigned, kindness and pure
knowledge (see D&C 121:41-42). He further says that when we

undertake to exercise control or dominion or compulsion upon the souls of the children of men, the heavens withdraw themselves and the Spirit of the Lord is grieved (see D&C 121:37).

If forcing our children to go to church is not the answer, then what is? This is one of those situations that is easier to prevent than to cure. We said earlier that there are some situations in which we do not present our children with alternatives. We matter-of-factly put the young child to bed at approximately the same time each night without asking him if he wants to go. In much the same way we take our children to church each week, except in cases of illness or for other extreme reasons, and they accept this just as they know that the sun rises and sets each day. We never make going to church a matter that is negotiable.

One of the authors feels fortunate in having been raised in a home wherein parents followed the practice suggested above. The question "Should we go to church today or not?" was never raised. If visitors arrived at an awkward time they were invited to come to church with us, but never did family members miss church to avoid offending the visitor. I can never remember any of us, in a family of ten children, ever refusing to go to church. In following my parents' example, I cannot recall any of my eight children rebelling about church attendance.

When resistance to church attendance does occur, parents may have not provided a *consistent* pattern of regular church attendance, or they may have been very autocratic and not given the child opportunities to make appropriate choices in other areas. In an attempt to be "his own person" the child may come to oppose the parents and adopt contrary behavior. If he feels the need to punish the parents for real or imagined over-control, he can really "hit them where it hurts" by refusing to go to church. Smoking, drinking, using drugs, and engaging in sexual activities are other ways teenagers find to punish or embarrass their parents.

Should one of your children reject the gospel, stop attend-
ing church, or adopt habits or practices that are contrary to
Church teachings, your best hope of returning him to the faith
is to continue to love him, accept him, and treat him as much
like the other children as possible. If you can maintain a good
relationship, there is a very good chance that he will recognize
his errors and repent of them.

Let Your Child Plan for His Own Future

When he was in high school and college, Ray Carlson
wanted to be a medical doctor. But because of financial diffi-
culties and other problems, he was never able to go to medical
school. From the time his oldest son, Richard, was born, Ray
has been determined that the boy will become a doctor. Now
that Richard is in junior high school his father's communications are not, "Well, son, have you thought about what you
might want to do in life?" but, "When you get into medical
school...." or, "Math is important because you'll need it in
your pre-med program." Richard has never been given any
choice in the matter. If he should rebel and go into another
major, or if he tries medical courses and is not successful, he
will probably have a deep feeling of guilt for "letting his father
down."

Parents need to be available and willing to give advice
about vocational choices, but they have no right to make
children's choices for them. A man who is in a profession or
business and would like to see his son follow in his footsteps
would do well to refrain from putting pressures upon the boy.
If he enjoys his work and is seen as happy and successful, there
is every chance that his son will elect the same vocation.

It is bad enough when a father puts pressure on his son to
take over his business or practice. But it is even worse when
the pressure is to something that the father himself *didn't* do,
as in the case of Ray Carlson. A parent has no right to force a
child to take some course of action to fulfill the parent's unful-
filled dream. The father may rationalize his own lack of
success when in reality he may not have had the aptitude for

the field. Now he tries to force his son, who may lack both aptitude and interest, to fulfill his life's dream vicariously.

A newspaper article told of a man who fulfilled his father's dream by becoming a lawyer, even though he really wanted to be a musician. After practicing in the profession for several years, probably hating every minute of it, he gave it all up and went back to music. What a waste of time, energy, and money! And what a lot of unhappiness could have been avoided in the first place had the father allowed him to be "his own person"!

To make important decisions for a child that he should make for himself is to rob him of his free agency and to say to him: "I am far wiser than you. I will tell you what to do; there is no need to think for yourself." Such an attitude robs the child of a feeling of capability and self-esteem.

Another important area of decision making is that of friends, and eventually an eternal marriage partner. It is painful to see a child forming alliances with children who are poor models of behavior and who violate gospel standards. When a child is very young you can control his friendships almost completely; but, like it or not, the older he gets the less control you can, or should, exert. Having taught your child a set of values, you hope he will make wise choices. If he identifies with you and internalizes your values, more often than not he will choose friends who exemplify those values; and when he does not, the relationship tends to be transitory.

The teenager is especially apt to resent attempts of parents to choose his friends. A teenager who feels a need to rebel against parents finds an excellent way to defy them by deliberately associating with people to whom the parents object. It is not a good idea to forbid your child to see a particular friend, since he is likely to go ahead and see the friend secretly. This gives you no control over where the association takes place or the kind of activities that go on. It would usually be better to encourage your child to invite his friends home and to be friendly with them. If the friend has characteristics or values that are different from those your child has grown up with, they are likely to stand out clearly against the backdrop of the home environment. In this situation the friend may lose some luster, and the relationship is more likely to be weakened.

We may sometimes long for the custom of other times and other places in which parents chose husbands and wives for their children. But, alas, our children do not like that idea at all and insist on choosing their own mates! The best guarantee that they will choose wisely is that they have been taught important values in a gospel perspective and that these values have been internalized.

Respect Your Child's Ideas

Let your child know that his ideas are interesting and important to you. You are a very good sounding board for him. Practice such comments as: "Hey, that's really good thinking." "I like that idea." "That's an interesting point of view." "I agree with you." Avoid being too critical. After all, you should not expect your child to be on an adult level in thinking and reasoning abilities. If you ridicule your child's ideas, or make light of them, you can be sure that the child will stop sharing them with you, and you will lose the opportunity to communicate with him. Furthermore, he may say to himself, "I don't know too much," or, "I'm not too bright," and such an attitude will negatively affect feelings of self-esteem.

Summary

In this chapter we have recommended that you help your child to move gradually from complete dependency at infancy to almost complete autonomy at young adulthood. At any stage along the way there are some decisions you must make for your child—those involving his safety and well-being. But the more decisions you can leave to him, the more his feelings of capability and self-esteem will be enhanced. One of the best ways to teach decision making is to be a good example of decision making yourself. It is also good to help your child to explore alternatives. Your child should be taught to involve the Lord, and, when appropriate, Church leaders, in his decisions, but not to expect either the Lord or others to make decisions for him. By your example, teach church attendance and adherence to gospel principles. Give your child advice in important life decisions, especially when he actively seeks it, but don't try to make the decisions for him. As you respect your child's ideas and teach him to think for himself, you contribute greatly to his feelings of capability and self-esteem.

Give Your Child Freedom to Express Negative Feelings

11

"Let every man be swift to hear, slow to speak, slow to wrath: For the wrath of man worketh not the righteousness of God"
(James 1:19-20).

What should you do if your young child, frustrated and in a fit of passion, should say, "I hate you!"

Should you cry and say, "How can you say such a naughty thing and make Mommy feel so bad?" Should you say: "You ungrateful little brat! Well, I hate you too!" Should you spank him, or wash his mouth out with soap? Or should you try to talk him out of his feelings by a comment, such as "Oh, you couldn't hate your very own mother!" At the moment he really feels the hatred, and probably the best thing to do would be to remain calm and make some comment, such as "You're really mad at me, aren't you?" Almost before you know it, your child will have forgotten that he was ever angry and will be coming to you for a cookie or a hug.

Suggestions for Dealing With Children's Negative Feelings

This section outlines a few of the ways to minimize the harmful effects of negative emotions upon your children. If you conscientiously apply these methods, your children's emotional health will be maintained and their self-concepts enhanced:

1. *Let your child know that negative feelings are normal and that all people have them.* Accept negative feelings, bring-

ing them out into the open rather than causing them to be hidden and repressed. Do not embarrass your child because of his bad feelings, and avoid ridicule. Ridicule and embarrassment are very ineffective ways of changing behavior, and they contribute to low self-esteem.

2. *Model good control of negative emotions for your child.* It is good for children to realize that "parents are people too." If mom and dad at times feel angry or sad or fearful, then maybe it isn't so bad for the children to have these feelings too. Of course, it is very important for parents to model effective ways of coping with these feelings. If a child sees a parent losing emotional control, saying cruel things to get even, lashing out physically or verbally, or otherwise displaying immature emotional behavior, he may deal with emotional stress in the same way.

3. *Give your child the right to his own feelings.* Too often parents try to talk children out of their feelings with statements, such as "Oh, big boys like you aren't afraid of the dark!" "You don't really hate your sister!" It would be much better to accept their feelings in a nonjudgmental way: "Yes, the dark basement is a little scary, isn't it?" "Sometimes even people we love do bad things and make us feel we dislike them." It's good for your child to know that in growing up it's normal to feel anger, hate, or jealousy at times, though we need to learn to control the expression of those feelings.

Sometimes parents or teachers force children to apologize, say they are sorry when they really aren't. This is not a good thing to do. Apologies need to be sincere and voluntary, based on the child's recognition of his own wrongdoings. Forced apologies are meaningless and cause resentment. They are also demeaning and work against self-esteem.

4. *Provide socially acceptable outlets for emotional feelings.* It is your child's *behavior* that needs to be restrained and controlled, not his feelings. Don't punish your child for being angry or fearful or jealous. Let him talk about how he feels and "get it off his chest." This is one of the best ways to reduce emotional tension. Use other ways of helping him to let out his feelings without hurting himself or others. "You can't hit your

little brother, but maybe it will make you feel better to punch this pillow." "I can't let you throw snowballs at people, but let's put this target up on the side of the garage and see how many bull's-eyes you can make!"

5. *Learn to really listen to your child.* Many parents would do well to talk less and listen more. Try to remember how you felt when you were a child in an adult-dominated world. Weren't there times when you felt misunderstood, mistreated? Weren't there times when you said to yourself: "Mom and Dad don't ever listen to me. They don't care about my feelings. They've forgotten what it's like to be young." How did you feel when parents or other adults made light of feelings that were very strong and important to you?

As you listen to the words your child says, try to understand the real feeling behind the words. You won't always be able to agree with these feelings, but let your child know that he has a right to feel that way.

Many counselors use with their clients a technique called active listening or reflective listening. Parents can also learn to employ this highly effective approach. In reflective listening we try to reflect the child's feelings with a comment that lets him know we understand. It is important that we do not just parrot the exact *words* that are spoken. Consider this example:

Kathy (coming home from Sunday school): "I don't like Sister Luke!"

Mom: "You don't like your teacher?"

Kathy: "She makes me so mad sometimes!"

Mom: "Sister Luke gets you really mad sometimes?"

Kathy: "And she's not really fair either."

Mom: "You feel that your teacher is not really fair."

Obviously, Kathy's mother is not doing reflective listening properly because she is just parroting her daughter's words. If she keeps this up, Kathy is likely to become irritated and say, "Mom, why are you repeating everything I say?"

If mother uses reflective listening in the correct way, the conversation might go like this:

Kathy: "I don't like Sister Luke!"

Mom: "Your teacher said something or did something to upset you?"

Kathy: "Ya. She really made me mad in class today. When I raised my hand, she just ignored me and always called on Marcie."

Mom: "She plays favorites, and that doesn't seem fair to you?"

Kathy: "That Marcie is such a snob, and all the teachers think she's a little angel."

Mom: "Marcie seems to think that she's better than you?" By continuing to reflect Kathy's feelings, mother encourages her to keep talking, and Kathy appreciates the fact that mom understands her; and eventually the real problem emerges.

What if mother's initial response had been: "Oh, you shouldn't feel that way about Sister Luke, she's really an excellent teacher"! A lecturing statement of this kind would be much less effective in getting at the problem than the reflective listening approach which the mother used. Good active listening lets your child know that you understand his feelings; and this understanding boosts his feelings of importance and self-esteem.

6. *Help your child to overcome unnecessary fears.* Karl, age ten, was asked by his mother to go down to the cellar and bring up some potatoes for dinner. When he didn't seem to have heard the request, his mother asked again. Karl got angry with his mother, saying that he had to do everything and asking why his brother couldn't do something once in a while. Karl's mother was puzzled by her son's overreaction to what seemed to be a logical and very simple request. It took her some time to realize that Karl was using anger as a way of covering up his real emotion—a fear of the dark, damp cellar. He didn't want his mother to scoff at his fears, and maybe even call him a baby. Anger was less of a threat to his self-esteem than fear.

Sometimes, as in the case of Karl, the cause of a child's fear is hidden. Once we know the cause we can take constructive steps to overcome the problem.

One approach to helping children overcome fears is to use a process called conditioning. Since fears often develop because the object or situation is associated with something the child already fears, we can reverse the process by associating the object or situation with something that is satisfying or enjoyable. Take the case of Karl, for example. He learned to fear the cellar because it was associated with darkness. His parents might do a series of very fun activities with him in the cellar until he associates it with fun, pleasant things rather than with darkness.

Another way of helping a child to overcome a fear is to give him more control over his environment. Paul, age three, was frightened at the sound of the noisy toilet in his bathroom. His mother found that if she let him be the one to push the handle and make the noise, rather than let the sound of flushing catch him off guard, his fear was eliminated. Paul's older brother was afraid of going to bed and imagined that there were monsters lurking in the shadows. His father solved the problem by giving him a new flashlight to keep right by his pillow, so that when he began to be frightened he could turn on the flashlight and assure himself that there was nothing threatening in the room.

A third way of helping a child to eliminate fear is to use negative adaptation. We force the child to face up to the situation until he gets used to it and loses his fear. This method should be used only when the fear is mild; you should not force your child into any situation that involves intense fear. The concept of sink or swim may work very well with a child who has only a mild fear of the water; but if you try it with a child who has an intense fear, you may have to pull him out of the water, dripping and screaming, to save his life. Furthermore, he may never go near the water again.

7. *Help your child to cope with anger.* The harmful effects of anger upon a child's feelings of self-esteem are not as obvious as the effects of fear. However, any negative emotion can interfere with a person's feelings of lovability and capability.

Very frequently anger is associated with frustration; when a child is prevented from doing something he wants to do, anger is a natural result. Even if you could prevent all frustration in a child's life, it would not be wise to do so. By coping with mild frustrations early in life, he learns to deal with the more serious ones he will face later. Though you should be careful about smoothing your children's way too much, you need to help him to cope with frustrations that are too serious or complex to deal with alone.

An early psychologist suggested that parents provide a fenced-in backyard, and then dig many holes for the child to crawl in and out of like an obstacle course. His idea was that this way the child would learn to handle adversity from the beginning of his life. Today we see this as naive and ill-advised. We don't have to deliberately set up frustrating situations for our children; life itself provides more than enough frustration. While we may wish it were possible to spare our children all frustrating, anger-provoking situations, our allowing them to work through their own problems helps them develop feelings of competence and self-esteem.

When your child is angry, it is important to maintain your own composure. The Bible says, "A soft answer turneth away wrath: but grievous words stir up anger" (Proverbs 15:1). Talk quietly and calmly, and try not to raise your voice. Do not let your child get you into a power struggle. If you should impulsively say or do something that you regret when the emotion is past, don't be afraid to admit your error and to apologize. Your child will feel more, not less, respect for you when you honestly admit mistakes.

Sometimes the best thing to do when your child is angry is to quietly remove yourself from the scene. If your young child throws a temper tantrum, usually the best thing to do is to simply walk out of the room and busy yourself in another part of the house. Few children can manage to continue a temper tantrum without an audience. Poor ways to handle the situation would be to punish the child for the tantrum, try to talk him out of it, or, worst of all, give in to the child.

Sometimes a "time-out" approach can be used to help an angry, aggressive child. In this approach you remove the child from the situation (take him to another room, for example) to provide a "cooling-off" period. This removal should be done as quietly and inconspicuously as possible to avoid either embarrassment or undue attention. Ideally, the child should not see the removal as a punishment, but as a chance for him to rest and regain self-control. A parent who says: "Get out of my sight, you little monster—you're mean and nasty and don't deserve to associate with normal human beings!" is not using the time-out approach. It would be much better to say: "You're really upset. You need a little time to cool down and get yourself under control." The time-out procedure should be used only for short time periods; and the younger the child, the shorter the time should be, perhaps only a matter of minutes in some cases. Then follow the advice of the Lord: "Reproving betimes with sharpness, when moved upon by the Holy Ghost; and then showing forth afterwards an increase of love . . . lest he esteem thee to be his enemy" (D&C 121:43).

8. *Help your child to cope with jealousy.* The emotion of jealousy involves love, fear, and anger. A person is fearful that he is losing love, and angry at whoever is perceived as the cause. The threat of losing love has obvious effects upon a person's self-esteem.

It is almost inevitable that there will be some jealousy among children in a family—especially between the oldest and the next oldest. When a child has been used to a "center-stage" position in the home, and suddenly an intruder enters the picture and takes away some of the attention that the child has come to see as his rightful due, is it any wonder that he asks if they can't return or otherwise get rid of the baby?

A good way to prevent jealousy is to see that each child gets his share of attention. At the advent of a baby, the toddler psychologically requires *more* attention all of a sudden—not less. As the infant nurses at the mother's breast, instead of constantly cooing and commenting about how sweet and beautiful the baby is, the mother would do well to notice and talk to the young child who is standing by watching. This is a good time for father to play an active role, either by doing things with the older child while mother cares for the baby, or by freeing her to spend time with the older child by caring for the infant himself. Blessed is the wife who has a husband who will change diapers and otherwise share in the parenting!

If you should visit a home in which there is a new baby and also a toddler or preschool child, pay some attention to the older child. If you bring a baby present, bring some small item for the other child—a small toy, or even a lollipop, is all that is needed.

Another good way for a parent to prevent jealousy is to include the older child in the situation. Refer to the infant as "our baby" instead of "my baby." Let the child help by bringing the baby's rattle, or by shaking baby powder on after the baby's bath.

Probably the best way to minimize jealousy in your home is to treat all of your children fairly, consistently, and as equally as possible. No matter how fair and equal your treatment, there are sure to be times when your children think they are being dealt with unjustly or that others in the family are receiving preferential treatment. But you can minimize such feelings by avoiding invidious comparisons and by helping each child to feel important in his own right.

Summary

In this chapter we have discussed ways of helping children to accept and express their feelings. They need to know that negative emotions are normal and common to all human beings, but they also need to learn to express these feelings in ways that are as socially acceptable as possible. Children need to find proper outlets for emotional feelings, not "bottle" them up inside. They need to see parents and other responsible adults handling their negative feelings in socially acceptable and productive ways. You should accept your child's feelings and not expect him to always think and feel as you do. Avoid forced apologies. Listen to your children empathetically and help them to feel understood. The chapter concludes with some specific suggestions for helping children to cope with the negative emotions of fear, anger, and jealousy.

Encourage Creativity in Your Child

12

"The honour of kings is to search out a matter. The heaven for height, and the earth for depth."
(Proverbs 25:2-3.)

Creativity is a God-given endowment that is present in varying degrees in all children. But too often adults stifle this creativity rather than foster it. Our schools in many ways do more to "turn off" the child than they do to stimulate his curiosity and desire to learn. The typical child enters kindergarten excited and anxious to learn. But by the third or fourth grade too many children have lost much of their native curiosity, interest, and enthusiasm. Teachers want children to learn the accumulated wisdom of the ages. But creativity involves *divergent thinking* in which a person goes off on tangents and thinks about something in his own unique way. This type of thinking is probably what got Edison and Einstein into trouble with their schoolteachers, causing them to be labeled "stupid" and "unteachable." Without divergent thinking nothing new would be invented.

The creative person is one who sees things around him in fresh, new ways. Rigid, inflexible people cannot be creative. Only a small percentage of people in the world will produce great works of music, art, and literature. But creativity can be expressed in many regular activities to add zest and enjoyment to life.

The Relationship of Creativity to Self-esteem

There is a strong relationship between creativity and self-esteem. Most creative children have a high degree of initiative, self-confidence, and independence. To be really creative, children must believe in themselves and be willing to accept the risk of trying out new things.

A child with low self-esteem is apt to stifle creative or unique ideas because of fear of disapproval and an inability to trust his own judgment. Conformity is not as much fun as creativity, but it is much safer.

The type of home environment that children experience has much to do with how efficiently they think and how creative they become. Parents can use techniques that stimulate a child's imagination and creativity, or they can resort to child-rearing practices that tend to stifle these characteristics.

Suggestions for Enhancing Creativity in Children

Following are some suggestions for encouraging children's creativity.

1. *Create a home that is democratic and to a degree even permissive.* Obviously, we cannot be so permissive as to fail to promote and enforce the living of gospel principles in the home. But beyond the keeping of God's commandments, there are a multitude of choices that we can either arbitrarily impose on our children or allow them to make for themselves. Creative expression is exhibited much more abundantly in children who are allowed freedom of thought and action than in children who are continually told how to think, feel, and behave. Many children from autocratic homes become model citizens, but few become known for their artistic and creative endeavors.

2. *Through praise and positive reinforcement, reward your child for his creative efforts.* One of the authors visited a first-grade class wherein there was an exhibit of children's art. He was amazed at the quality of the work displayed and thought that it must be the work of some of the more advanced or gifted children, but was told that every child in

the class had three pictures displayed. When asked her secret in helping children to do such outstanding art work, the teacher replied something like this: "Well, I don't have much art ability myself, so I sort of just turn them loose to paint what they want. I never say anything negative, but I look for something positive about the drawing that I can compliment the child about. For example, if a child fills the whole sheet instead of just drawing a little object in one corner, I tell him how pleased I am that he used the whole paper." Contrast this wise teacher with another elementary schoolteacher who displayed a picture of a fruit bowl and had everyone in the class make one exactly like it, criticizing one child who substituted an orange for an apple, and another child who drew the banana at a different angle from the one in the model.

You should compliment your child about the positive aspects of his art. Hang his pictures up on the wall, and prominently display other creative works in the home. You will want to save some samples of creative work that your child does at different ages. How interesting it will be for him as an adult to be able to see them! Since it will not be practical to save everything, you will have to dispose of some of your child's creations. But be sure to do it inconspicuously. Never let him come home and find something he has done thrown carelessly in the trash can.

3. *Avoid negative criticism or ridicule of your child's artistic work.* Jenny, age five, approached her father, who was reading a newspaper, to show him a crayon drawing she had made. Enticed reluctantly from his paper, he looked at the picture and asked, "What's that?" She replied, "A little girl and a dog." He said, "I never saw a dog that looked like that!" and quickly resumed his reading. He failed to see Jenny quietly crumple up her picture and throw it into the fireplace. What an effective way to stifle a child's creative impulses and lower her self-esteem!

While few parents, fortunately, are as insensitive as Jenny's father, we may inadvertently stifle creativity in subtle ways. Even the question, "What's that?" may discourage a child. A much better thing to say when a child shows you a drawing is, "Tell me about your picture." In this way you avoid letting the child know you can't tell what it is supposed to be and you prevent the discouragement that might otherwise result.

4. *Encourage initiative and creative exploration in your child.* The Lord said: "For behold, it is not meet that I should command in all things; for he that is compelled in all things, the same is a slothful and not a wise servant.... Verily I say, men should be anxiously engaged in a good cause, and do many things of their own free will . . . For the power is in them, wherein they are agents unto themselves." (D&C 58:26-28.) Likewise, we should not try to tell our children every move to make, but leave them free to decide and do many things on their own. There is a temptation for parents to try to protect children too much, discouraging any exploration that has any messiness, discomfort, or inconvenience associated with it. To do so is to curtail a child's initiative, and possibly exert a negative influence upon creativity and feelings of self-esteem.

5. *Respect your child's thoughts, suggestions, and ideas.* Accept the child's ideas without ridiculing them, but do not make him self-conscious with your amazed comment or lavish praise. Some parents encourage the child to show off, making him vain and self-conscious and spoiling true creativity. Accepting your child's ideas and suggestions in a natural way will foster creative, independent thought. Comments, such as "I like that idea," or "That's good thinking," will help him feel capable and bolster his feelings of self-worth.

6. *Make creative materials available to your child.* Your home should contain a variety of materials to stimulate creativity in your children. Paper, scissors, clay, paints, paste, crepe paper, ribbons, colored fabric, blocks, sand, simple musical instruments, and educational toys and games are all helpful in stimulating imagination and providing opportunities for creative activity. Even a cardboard box or a carpet end tube can provide hours of amusement and creativity.

If creativity is to be fostered, you must be able to tolerate some degree of messiness and disorder *at times.* The rule "a place for everything, and everything in its place" may contribute to an efficient and orderly home. But it can be carried to an undesirable extreme, as shown in this example. Ten-year-old Theresa became restless and uncomfortable when a visitor who was waiting to see Theresa's mother picked up an ornament from the shelf to admire it and then set it down again. Finally the child came over and turned the object in the other direction, saying, "Mother won't like it if it's turned the wrong way." While there is no virtue in general disorder and untidiness, a rigid home like Theresa's is not likely to be conducive to creativity.

7. *Have fun with your children and participate with them in interesting activities.* Introduce variety into your family home evening activities. Involve your children in games and activities which stimulate creative thought and action. Take bicycle and nature walks, and talk about the interesting things you see along the way. Visit manufacturing plants, radio and television studios, bakeries, police and fire stations, and similar attractions to broaden experience and stimulate interest. Encourage activities such as rhythmic dancing, singing, dramatics, and modeling.

8. *Help your children to be sensitive to the beauties around them.* Sit beside them and observe a beautiful sunset, a waterfall, snow gently falling, waves dashing against the shore, the moon appearing to move as the clouds pass by its face, the stars shining in the sky at night. Talk about how these things make you feel, and encourage children to do the same.

9. *Help your children to develop their imagination and intuitive powers.* The young child lives and breathes in a world of imagination. But with age there is a tendency for imagination to be suppressed by others and by the demands of the environment. You need to be careful what your young child watches on television and in the movies, since children up to the age of five or six have difficulty in separating out what is real and what is not real. Strong emotions may be evoked by events on the screen which the child believes are really happening.

At seven or eight years of age children are generally able to distinguish pretty clearly between reality and imagination. But they enjoy pretending and will sometimes exaggerate the sights and sounds around them to spice up their lives. For example, Charley may see a very large yellow house cat and rush home to tell mom that he just saw a tiger out in the street. It is sometimes difficult to tell whether the child really believes his story. A parent may become overly concerned, convinced that unless this problem is nipped in the bud the child will grow up to be an inveterate liar. It is not a good idea to wash out your child's mouth with soap or otherwise punish him, or to make him feel guilty about his tall tales. Rather than stifle the creativity that is associated with these "lies," you might wink and smile, "Boy, Charley can sure make up good stories," or "You sure have a great imagination." The parent or teacher can even help him to write the story down and make a book, allowing him to draw pictures to illustrate it. This method of encouraging creative story telling, while letting your child know that you know the story is not true, encourages imagination and creativity without letting your child manipulate you.

10. *Make wise use of television in the home.* Television is a very potent learning tool, and children glean a great deal of information from it. It also helps shape their values. Unfortunately, a great deal of material on television is of questionable value, from the standpoint of both information and moral teachings. An LDS parent must continually monitor the family's viewing to see that questionable material is eliminated and useful material retained.

Television does very little to stimulate creativity and imagination. In the old days of radio drama a person had to visualize the characters and imagine the events of the story, as when reading a story or book. But with TV a person sees the characters directly and views the events on the screen as though they were actually happening, and there is little need for imagination.

There is some evidence that TV dulls the senses rather than

enlivening them. Constant viewing of crime and violence does not turn a normal person to violence or to a life of crime. But it does seem to desensitize a person to pain and human suffering. There have been accounts in the press of people standing by while someone else is raped or murdered, when even mild intervention might have saved the victim. People, it seems, are sometimes transfixed by the event, as though it were happening on a TV or movie screen.

It is important for you to control the type and amount of television viewing of your children. You may need to literally push them out of the door and encourage active, creative play situations. One of the authors remembers from childhood days how a ladder propped up on a wooden box with a board across it was transformed into an airplane, providing an imaginative play activity which lasted for hours. A hole dug in the vacant lot next door became a foxhole, a clubhouse, or a secret cave. Ropes tied to tree limbs became vines for Tarzan to swing on through the jungle. Activities such as these stimulate more creativity and imagination in children than does TV and the fresh air and exercise promote a higher degree of physical health and well-being.

11. *Allow ample time for your child to enjoy free play and just to be a child.* While it is vital for a child to have responsibilities and to learn how to work, it is also important that we do not plan so much of his time that there is little time left for free play and enjoyable activities. The demands of school, Church, and formal youth activities can become so great as to be almost overwhelming. Some parents expect children to function as "little adults" rather than as children. A child who continually takes on adultlike duties, never complains, works overtime to achieve high marks in school, and seldom has time for play is apt to be neither really happy nor creative.

12. *Help your child to accept mistakes and failures realistically.* Let your child know that making mistakes or failing at some things is part of being human. If the prospect of failure is too threatening for children, they may simply withdraw from the activity, feeling that it is better not to try at

all. Part of helping a child to accept mistakes and failures is to admit openly your own mistakes with comments, such as "Well, I really botched that!" or, "It looks like I was wrong about that." Such admissions help your children to realize that if even mom and dad fail at times, maybe its okay for them to fail too. Unless they are able to expose themselves to the risk of possible failure, they will not have the initiative and self-confidence needed for creative expression.

13. *Resist the temptation to say no to your child.* Too many restrictions can inhibit your child and stifle his initiative and creativity. Count the number of times you say "no" and "don't" to your young child each day, and you will understand why these words become so common in the child's own vocabulary. If you say "don't" too often, it may either lose its effectiveness or inhibit your child to the point that he is afraid to try almost anything.

Obviously, there are many times when we must legitimately restrict children's activities, but before we say no we need to ask ourselves "Why not?" or, "What difference will it make?" We will often find that there is really no defensible reason for not allowing the child to do the thing that is in question.

14. *Answer your child's questions on a level he can understand.* Questions grow out of children's curiosity, and the way we answer them can either help the curiosity to grow or cause it to be repressed. Avoid the temptation to tell your child everything you know about the subject, thus overwhelming and confusing him. Answer simply, on the child's level. If you don't know the answer to a question, don't bluff, but freely admit that you don't know. Parents do not have to project an image of infallibility and omniscience for their children. This would be an excellent time to say, "Why don't we look that up in the encyclopedia?" or, "Let's see what we can find in the scriptures or the writings of the General Authorities."

It is often a good idea to answer a child's question with a question: "What do you think?" or, "Do you have any ideas about that?" This procedure will help you to see what level of thinking your child is capable of. Children often surprise us with their insight. We should encourage them to use their powers of creative thinking and reasoning rather than simply being open vessels into which we pour knowledge.

Summary

This chapter emphasizes the importance of creativity and the contribution it makes to self-esteem. Parents respond to children in ways that can either enhance or inhibit creativity. Fourteen ways of enhancing creativity are discussed. If you will make a conscientious effort to follow these suggestions, you are almost certain to stimulate your child's creativity and build his feelings of capability and self-esteem.

Take Time for Training

13

*"Train up a child in the way he should
go: and when he is old, he will not depart
from it"*
(Proverbs 22:6).

"Hey, Al, when are you going to get around to pruning
that peach tree?"

"Oh, well, Frank, I tried, but it's a beautiful tree, and I
can't stand to see it mutilated by cutting off all those
branches."

Al is so tenderhearted that his peach tree will never rise to
its true potential. When it comes time to thin the fruit, he can't
bring himself to pick those tiny peaches before their time and
throw them on the ground. The fruit is so crowded and shaded
that at maturity the peaches are less than half the size they
should be.

Children are a bit like trees. The time to train a tree so that
it has the right number of branches all going in the right direction is while it is quite small. "As the twig is bent..." is a
familiar statement and a very true one. The time to train a
child is also when he is quite small. Young branches growing in
the wrong place on a tree can be removed with the thumbnail;
if allowed to grow for a few years, the branches become so
large that it takes strenuous effort to remove them, and ugly
scars are left. Negative traits in a child are also eliminated most

easily when the child is young; if allowed to persist till maturity, the traits may be so well established as to be almost impossible to change. Perhaps it is no accident that we refer to both places that raise trees and places that care for young children as nurseries.

A well-known poem by an author I have not been able to identify also stresses the importance of early training.

A Piece of Clay

I took a piece of plastic clay
And idly fashioned it one day.
And as my fingers pressed it, still
It moved and yielded to my will.

I came again when days were past;
The bit of clay was hard at last.
The form I gave it still it bore,
And I could fashion it no more!

I took a piece of living clay,
And gently pressed it day by day,
And moulded with my power and art
A young child's soft and yielding heart.

I came again when years had gone;
It was a man I looked upon.
He still that early impress bore,
And I could fashion it no more!

Teach Your Children Proper Church Behavior

"No, Marcie! You're going to tear the hymnbook holding it that way!" "George, don't let Mark crawl under the benches!" "Hey, you two, cut that out! We don't fight in church!" "Joan, put that book away! You're old enough to listen to the talks." "Steven, get right back here! Church will be out in ten more minutes, and you can certainly wait that much longer."

It seems to Sister Clark that most of her time in sacrament meeting is spent in disciplining her five children—telling them to be quiet, refereeing their arguments, keeping them on the benches, and encouraging them to listen. She is embarrassed by their behavior and concerned about what other members of the congregation are thinking about the family. Each week she asks herself if it is really worth it and swears to herself that next week she will stay home with the youngest, most unmanageable family members.

Contrast this family with another family in the ward with five children of approximately the same ages. The oldest son, age fourteen, and daughters ages ten and eleven, each bring a small notebook to church and take notes of the main ideas that are expressed. When the family gets home the father and mother encourage the children to compare notes of what they learned from each talk, and dad and mom add their own contributions. In this way each family member is paying more attention in church and getting more out of the meetings. Because of the good training given by the parents and the good example of older brother and sisters, the four-year-old boy and seven-year-old girl are easy to manage. They want to have their own notebooks, and even though the four-year-old's writing is just scribbles, it takes up some of his time and makes him feel part of the situation.

Which of these two families does yours most resemble? At best a parent's job is not easy, and in sacrament meeting it can be doubly hard. Brother and Sister Clark need to begin immediately to provide the training that their children need so that as they get older they will become church worshippers and not just people who take up space on the benches.

It is the authors' opinion that children who are too young to appreciate the church service or to comprehend the ideas being expressed need some extra support in the form of noiseless toys, treats, or picture books. But as they get old enough to listen and understand, they should be encouraged to pay attention.

If you train your older children to behave properly and pay attention to what is going on around them, your work with younger children becomes much, much easier. Older children in the family can serve as good role models in the same way that parents do.

Train Your Children to Work

"For the third time, please clean up your room!" said Mrs. Conn to her nine-year-old daughter. Yet an hour later Jeannette was still stretched out on her bed reading comic books. Mother became more and more upset and began to contemplate what kind of punishment would be appropriate for her daughter's laziness and disobedience.

Perhaps Jeannette is not really being either lazy or disobedient. She may not know quite where to begin or just how to proceed. Parents sometimes forget that tasks that seem relatively clear-cut and simple to an adult may seem confusing and overwhelming to a child. Another possibility is that Jeannette may know from past experience that no matter how hard she tries, mother will not be happy with her efforts. In either case, Mrs. Conn should provide training in order for her daughter to feel competent. It may be necessary for her to work side by side with Jeannette several times until she feels comfortable in doing it on her own. As she begins to feel more and more competent, both her willingness to work and her self-esteem will be fostered.

Take a Moderate Approach in Training Your Child

It takes time for a child to learn a new task. It would not be appropriate for you to expect the task to be done the way you would do it. On the other hand, if you just accept any slipshod, half-effort performance, you do your child no favor either.

Suppose you were to come home from the grocery store to find the table set for dinner, and your six-year-old daughter standing by with a big smile on her face. You notice that the positions of the forks and the spoons are reversed and that she has used a motley assortment of glasses. Think of the possible approaches that might be used, and the effect of each upon the child's self-esteem.

"You're a little too young yet to set the table. Here, let Mommy show you how."

"It just makes more work for me when you set the table and don't do it right. Now I have to get the silverware in the right places and put all the glasses back and get a matched set."

"Now, you know that Mommy has told you not to get glasses out of the cupboard by yourself. It's a wonder you didn't break one!"

How quickly you could take away the child's thrill at surprising you and deflate the child's ego by any of the above statements! The best approach at first would be to simply accept the child's actions in a very positive way and thank her for helping, saying nothing at all about the errors. Then, a little later or at another time, you could comment that it really looks nice when all the glasses are just alike and that usually the fork goes on the left side and the spoon on the right. The point is that in our zeal to see something done correctly, we should not overlook the fact that, after all, the child did take the initiative to perform the act in the first place.

Suggestions for Training Children

Following are some do's and don'ts that might be considered in training children:

1. *Institute training when the child is at an optimal stage of development.* This principle applies both to training of behaviors and to training of skills. There is little or no value in attempts to teach your child before he is ready. Interesting studies have been done with identical twins in which one twin was given intensive training in activities, such as roller skating or bicycle riding, at a very early age and the other was not. The typical finding is that later on when the untrained twin is allowed to try these activities, he very quickly catches up. The early training seems to have made little or no difference.

Some people feel that unless they start their children on piano lessons by the age of five or six, they are delinquent in their duties as parents. But unless the child has a very unusual aptitude for music, it is better to start lessons at about ten. At this age learning is much more rapid, and the child will in a

year or so be at the same level of competency as if he had
started several years earlier. Think of all the frustration that is
avoided when the child is old enough to make rapid progress,
and think how his feelings of capability and self-esteem are
promoted, not to mention the money that is saved by not
starting so early.

2. *Be patient.* Rome was not built in a day. In our time-
conscious world a parent is sometimes too busy to wait for the
inexperienced child to take twice as long as an adult to do a
task, so she chooses to do it the "easy way" by doing it herself.
If this situation is repeated time after time, the child may
develop real or feigned feelings of inadequacy and know that if
he dawdles or says he doesn't know how, mom or dad will
come to the rescue. Be willing to wait for the child to do what
you have asked him to do. Don't take pity on him and do it
yourself because you can do it more quickly and more efficiently. When the task is finished, if the child has put forth a
good effort thank him for helping. By all means avoid the
temptation to tell him all the parts of the task that were done
incorrectly. Expect slow, but regular, improvement on future
occasions.

3. *Make learning and work fun.* "Come on, kids! Let's see
who can gather up the most papers that have blown around
the yard."

"Hey, this living room really looks a mess! Tell you what,
the first one to pick up ten things and put them where they
belong gets the biggest piece of strawberry shortcake!"

"Let's see how many earthworms we can find while we dig
up the garden!"

"When you get through weeding the carrots, I'm going to
come and inspect. If I can't find more than five weeds, you win
the prize!"

To quote a line from *Mary Poppins*, "Just a spoonful of
sugar helps the medicine go down." Your child will learn
something that is pleasant and fun much more quickly than if
it is distasteful. But, of course, it is not possible or advisable to
sugarcoat everything that the child does. There is something to

be said for teaching your child to persevere in the face of adversity and complete work that he does not enjoy doing. There will be plenty of those situations in his life. But to teach him to get enjoyment out of his work is to do him a favor that may enrich his life forever.

4. *Simplify the task by breaking it down into smaller steps.* The task of doing the dishes may seem confusing and overwhelming to a young child. But he may handle one part of the job very well. If you teach him the sequential steps that are involved, the work becomes comprehensible: First, we bring all the dishes from the table to the sink; next, we rinse them and then stack them neatly on the cupboard next to the sink; next, we wash the dishes with hot soapy water and rinse them in hot water; and so on. Breaking the task into steps also allows us to divide the responsibility among two or three children and to promote cooperation among family members. The simpler aspects of the task can be assigned to the younger members of the family, and they can feel the same sense of completion and competency that older family members enjoy.

5. *Choose a good time for training.* When you or your child is tired or out of sorts, postpone the training session to a better time. When he is pleased with something he has done on his own, this is not the time to minimize his contribution by saying, "Let me show you how to do it right." When your young child misbehaves in the supermarket or in church, and you have to remove him from the scene as quickly and unobtrusively as possible, the situation is too emotionally charged to be a good time for teaching acceptable behavior. Choose a quiet time when you are unhurried and free from emotion.

Summary

In this chapter we have stressed the role of the parent as a teacher. The two main areas that are discussed are (1) helping your children to behave properly in church and (2) training them to work. We emphasized the value of early training, stressing that expectations should be reasonable and appropriate for your child's level of readiness. If you begin too early, learning will be ineffective; if you wait too long, the child's interest may have passed to other matters and may be difficult to reactivate. Be patient and realize that it will take your child longer to do a task than if you were to do it, and it will probably be done less well. Your being too critical can discourage your child and decrease his feelings of competency and self-esteem.

Simplify tasks by breaking them down into smaller steps. Work shoulder to shoulder with your child when the task is too difficult for him to do alone. Keep your sense of humor and try to make learning and work fun. Time the training sessions to fit the situation and the moods of you and your child. As your child learns to behave properly in church and in other social situations, and as he learns to do assigned tasks well, his feelings of self-worth will grow.

Conclusion   14

*"He that endureth to the end shall be
saved"*
(Matthew 10:22).

It is the authors' hope that you have been able to apply
some of the specific suggestions made throughout the book.
Since parents, like children, are all different, you have no
doubt found some suggestions to be more appropriate and
easy to apply than others. Try to implement those techniques
that make most sense to you, and, at least for now, don't
worry about the others.

As a concerned parent, you are probably already doing
many of the things we have mentioned in this book. But
reminders can be helpful. After all, we go to church week after
week, and very little of what we hear is really new. Just as we
leave a stirring sacrament meeting with a resolve to apply the
principles that were discussed, so the authors hope that this
book will help you in your resolve to be the best parent you
know how to be. Use it as a reference source and consult it as
the need arises, and you will become more effective in the enhancement of your children's self-esteem.

Suggestions for Getting the Most From This Book

Of the following procedures choose those that seem most
reasonable and that best fit your personality, and then make a
real attempt to follow through with them:

1. *Review the book often.* Glance over the italicized passages and topic headings. Read the summaries at the end of each chapter.

2. *Identify the suggestions that fit your situation best.* As you read or review the book, have a paper and pencil handy and jot down the suggestions that seem to be most relevant to your family.

3. *Set priorities.* Don't try to work on too many things at once or you may confuse your children and yourself. Benjamin Franklin is said to have been very effective in self-improvement. He would pick one virtue at a time and work on it for a specified period before taking on another. You may wish to try a similar method. Decide what procedures are most important, and then set to work to implement them.

4. *Work as a team.* Parents who work at cross purposes with each other can defeat the best procedures and techniques. Once you and your spouse have made decisions involving your children, support each other's decisions even though you think other decisions might have been better, and then talk it over in private later. Be sure not to let your children manipulate the situation and set you at odds with each other.

If parents see things in about the same way and are willing to work cooperatively to enhance the self-esteem of their children, the battle is already half won. Decide together what is most important, and then do it. Suppose that you and your spouse decide that you shout at your children too much. You can help each other to change by giving quiet reminders at critical times. A little private signal can be helpful.

5. *Go easy on yourself.* Many times in our interactions with children we do not have time to sit down and calmly review all alternatives and possible consequences. We are apt to react impulsively or by habit. Later on we may realize that another approach would probably have been better. Fortunately, effective parenting does not require perfection. Children are resilient and can take normal foibles and inconsistencies in their stride. When you "goof," face up to the situation and resolve to let it be a learning experience. Don't be afraid to apologize to your children when the situation really

calls for it. But don't become self-depreciating or self-demeaning. Remember that you are the most important model for your children, especially those of the same sex. Recognize your human imperfections, but like and respect yourself in spite of them. Then help your children to do the same.

6. *Don't give up on an idea or technique too quickly.* When we try something new and it does not immediately work out, there is a temptation to give up and revert to the old method, saying, "I just knew that idea wasn't practical and would never work!" Remember, just as you know your children and can often anticipate their behavior, so they have learned to anticipate your actions and cope with your methods of child care. When your actions change, children are likely to become confused. When a specific behavior that has had "payoff" for your child no longer works, the child's efforts are likely to be redoubled, and things will probably become worse for a short time before they get better.

"Please, Mom, can I go over to Susan's and see their kittens?" "Terri, I told you that I want you to get your homework done before you go anywhere." If mom has a reputation for meaning what she says, that is probably where the dialogue ends. Terri knows enough not to ask again until the homework has been completed.

But if mom has been known in the past to vacilate and be indecisive, the conversation may continue as follows:

"Please, Mom, *please!*" (spoken with such feeling that you would suppose her very life depended upon seeing those kittens).

"You may go after your homework is finished, if it isn't too late."

"But, Mom, it will be too late; that mean Mrs. Madsen gave us so much homework."

The dialogue continues on and on until finally mother says in exasperation, "Well, if it's *that* important to you, go ahead. But you'd better be back in twenty minutes."

Mother has lost the battle again; her beautiful resolve to remain firm and not let Terri manipulate her is gone once again. Terri knows that if she just persists long enough, mom will get tired of resisting and let her do what she wants to do. Terri has learned to be importunate rather than obedient. Mother has to learn to say no to Terri and mean it. There is no need to get mean or nasty with her daughter; she should simply and firmly refuse to debate the issue any longer. She should busy herself with her own affairs and stop responding to Terri's pleadings. If her daughter follows her from room to room she can always retreat to the one place she cannot follow—the bathroom—and lock the door.

Once you decide to try something new with your children, be persistent and give it time to work. Once they see that you mean business and that the ground rules have really changed, they will change accordingly.

7. *Seek your Father in Heaven's advice and help.* The principles discussed in this book are true, but they must be applied differently from one family to another, and even one child to another. Few things in your life are as important as your relationships with your children. Your Father in Heaven wants you to be successful in your endeavors as a parent. Pray daily for inspiration to guide you in this important calling. With his help how can you fail?

It's Never too Late

If you are a young parent, you have a real advantage in learning to apply important principles of child care and self-esteem enhancement. If you are an older parent whose children are almost raised, you may be tempted to say, "I wish I had tried some of these ideas when my children were young, but I guess it's too late to do much about it now." *It is not too late!* Self-esteem can be enhanced even in an adult. Start today to apply those principles that contribute to high self-esteem in you and in your children.

Index

— A —

Accomplishments, children's, 38-39
  See also Competence
Active listening, 76-77
Activities, family, 56, 58, 60
"Affect hunger," 37-38
Affection, display of, 37, 39
Agency, 68-69, 71
Allowances (money), 67-68
Anadarko, Oklahoma, 27
Anger, 13, 50
  coping with, 74, 75, 78-80
Antagonism, 43
Anxiety, 13
Apologies, forced, 75, 81
Art, 83-85

— B —

Babies, and jealousy, 80-81
Beauty, sensitivity to, 86
Bedtime, 59, 61, 64
Behavior, appropriate reinforcement,
    13-14
  church, 19-20, 92-94
  love used as control, 38
  objectionable, 53
Books, 29-30
Brown, Hugh B., 11

— C —

Capabilities, 38-39
Carnegie, Dale, 12
Child development norms, 20-22, 95-96
"Childproofing," 23-24
Children, and courtesy, 42-47
  creativity in, 82-90
  curiosity of, 22-24
  decision-making by, 62-73
  discipline of, 48-54
  feelings of importance, 12-18
  handicapped, 60
  individuality of, 57
  initiative of, 24-26
  love in, 36-41

loved by Jesus Christ, 55
  negative emotions in, 74-81
  parents' expectations for, 19-22
  time for, 55-61
  training in church behavior, 92-94
  training in service, 27-35
  training to work, 94-98
  See also Family, Fathers, Mothers,
    Parents
Christmas, 33
Church attendance, 68-70
Church behavior, 19-20, 92-94
Church leaders, inspiration through, 66
Church welfare program, 33
Clegg, William C., 68
Commandments, 41
Communication, emotional outlet, 5,
    75, 76-77
  parent/child, 29, 70, 72
Comparisons, invidious, 14-15
  sibling, 14-15, 38-39
  with other children, 20-22
Competence, self-esteem through, 4,
    19-26
  See also Accomplishments
Competition, effect on self-esteem,
    16-17
Compliments, 31, 36
Compulsion, 69
Conceit, 2-3
Conditioning, overcoming fear through,
    78
Confidence, 24-26, 65
Consequences, logical, 50-54
  natural, 50-54
Consideration, 8
  self-esteem through, 4-5, 42-47
Consolidated meeting schedule, 60-61
Counselors, 22, 76
Courage, 24-26, 30
Courtesy, self-esteem through, 4-5,
    42-47
Cowdery, Oliver, 66
Creative exploration, encouragement
  of, 85
Creative materials, 85-86
Creative play, 88

Creativity, encouragement of, 83-90
  self-esteem through, 5, 82-90
Criticism, 31
  of artistic work, 84-85
Curiosity, 22-24

— D —

Dating, 48-49
Decision-making, inspiration in, 66
  self-esteem through, 5, 62-73
  teaching skills of, 65
Decisions, children's, 62-73
Dependence, of children on parents,
    53, 64-65
  See also Independence
Devotion, 30
Discipline, of self, 49
  self-esteem through, 5, 48-54
  system of leadership, 49, 53-54
  through Holy Ghost, 50, 80
  See also Punishment
Discouragement, 20
Dispensation of fulness of times, 60
Divorce, effect on self-esteem, 37

— E —

Edison, Thomas A., 82
Einstein, Albert, 82
Embarrassment, avoidance of, 45-46,
    47, 80
  in expressing love, 36
  ineffective in changing behavior, 75
  loss of self-esteem through, 18
Emotional health, 30-31, 74-81
Emotions, handling of, 74-81
Envy, 14-15
Example, courtesy taught by, 42-43, 47
  decision-making taught by, 67, 72
  emotional control taught by, 75
  love taught by, 29, 41
  service taught by, 33-34
Expectations, parental, 19-26
Experimentation, importance to
    children, 22-24

— F —

Failure, acceptance of, 88-89
Family, activities, 56, 58, 60, 86
  home evening, 60-61, 86
  importance of, 56, 60
  prayer, 60
  pride, 60-61

service projects, 33-34
solidarity, 61
traditions, 61
  See also Children, Fathers, Mothers,
    Parents
Fasting, 20
Father, God as, 7
Fathers, 56, 58, 81
Fear, 9
  overcoming of, 77-78
Forgiveness, 9
Franklin, Benjamin, 100
Free agency, 68-69, 71
Freedom, creativity fostered by, 83
Friends, choice of, 71-72
Frustration, 78-79

— G —

Games, competitive, 16-17
Gifts, baby, 81
  Christmas, 33
  no substitute for self, 57, 61
God, as our Father, 7, 42
  becoming like, 8
  love for, 8, 40-41
  love of, 7
  spirit children of, 3, 42
Gossip, 29
Guilt, 38, 57, 88
  through misbehavior, 53
  through punishment, 49, 50

— H —

Handicapped children, 60
Hate, 29, 75
Health, emotional, 30-31, 74-81
Holy Ghost, discipline through, 50, 80
  See also Prayer
Honor, 30
Hostility, 13, 50
Housework, 58
*How to Win Friends and Influence
    People,* 12
Humility, 8, 10, 28
Humor, effect on self-esteem, 17-18
  sense of, 98

— I —

Imagination, 86-87
Independence, 53, 64-65
  development of, 24-26
  of creative children, 83

Initiative, development of, 24-26
  encouragement of, 85
  of creative children, 83
Inquisitiveness, 22-24
Inspiration, 66
  See also Holy Ghost, Prayer
Integrity, 30
Invidious comparisons, 14-15

— J —

Jealousy, coping with, 75, 80-81
Jesus Christ, 7-10, 28, 31
  love for children, 55
  self-esteem of, 10
Jorgenson, Glenn A., 30-31, 32
Joseph (Old Testament prophet), 15

— K —

Kimball, Spencer W., 27-28
Kindness, 8, 30
King Benjamin, 28
"Know This, That Every Soul Is Free"
  (hymn), 68

— L —

Leadership, best discipline, 49, 53-54
Learning, pleasant, 96-97
  readiness for, 19-22
Lee, Harold B., on home, 56
Listening, active, 76-77
  reflective, 76-77
Logical consequences, 50-54
Love, expression of, 37, 39-40
  fear of losing, 80
  for children, 70
  for God, 8, 40-41
  for others, 8-10, 36, 40-41
  of God, 7
  of others, 31-32, 34
  resistance to evil through, 9-10
  self-esteem through, 4, 36-41
  used as control of behavior, 38

— M —

McKay, David O., on home, 56
Manners, 42-43
Marriage, communication in, 59-60
  decision, 71-72
  love in, 36
Media, 29-30
Meekness, 8

Minorities, acceptance of, 30
Misbehavior, 53
Missionary experiences, 9-10, 27-28
Missions, money for, 67
Mistakes, acceptance of, 24, 88-89
  dealing with, 46
  learning through, 63, 68
Money management, 67-68
Moses, 10
Mothers, 58
Movies, 29-30, 58

— N —

Nagging, 43, 47
Natural consequences, 50-54
Negative adaptation, overcoming fear
  through, 78
Negative feelings, acceptable outlets
  for, 75-76, 81
  acceptance of, 74-75, 81
  control of, 75
Newspapers, 30, 58

— P —

Parents, cooperation between, 101
  example of, 29, 33-34, 41, 42-43,
    47, 67, 72, 75
  time for each other, 59-60
Patience, 25, 96
Paul (Apostle), 31
Perfection, achievement of, 8
Permissiveness, 53, 83
Persistence, 101-2
Physicians, 22
"Piece of Clay" (poem), 92
Pity, 52
Plan of salvation, self-esteem through
  knowledge of, 4, 7-11
Play, creative, 88
Play, free, 88
Positive Action Theory of Behavior,
  30-31, 32
Positive reinforcement, 13-14, 83-84
Praise, 14, 16, 25, 31, 83-84, 85
Prayer, 41, 66, 102
Premortal life, 68
Priesthood, 11
Priorities, 100
Professional help, 21-22
Promiscuity, 37-38
Prophets, 10
Psychologists, 22

Punishment, inappropriate for
  emotions, 75
  inappropriate for tantrums, 79
  only one aspect of discipline, 49-54
  See also Discipline

— Q —

Questions, answered with questions,
  89-90
Quiet time, 59, 61

— R —

Rebellion, 65, 69, 71
Reflective listening, 76-77
Reinforcement, positive, 13-14
Resentment, 13, 43, 62, 75
Respect, for children's ideas, 72, 73, 85
  for others, 42
  for parents, 49
Responsibility, 53
Restrictions, on children's activities, 89
Retaliation, 8-9
"Reverse gossiping," 30-31
"Reverse tattling," 30-31
Ridicule, devastating effect on self-
    esteem, 43, 47
  ineffective in changing behavior, 75
  loss of self-esteem through, 18
  of children's art, 84-85
  of children's ideas, 72, 85

— S —

Sarcasm, 43, 47
Satan, 60, 68
Schools, creativity stifled in, 82
Scolding, 43, 47
Scripture study, family, 61
Security, 37, 48-49, 61
Self-centeredness, 28
Self-confidence, 24-26, 65
  of creative children, 83
Self-discipline, 49
Self-esteem, and conceit, 2-3
  enhancement in children, 4-6
  in gospel perspective, 3
  of Jesus Christ, 10
  parents' role in, 1-2
  through communication of feelings,
    5, 74-81
  through competence, 4, 19-26
  through courteous treatment, 4-5,
    42-47

through creativity, 5, 82-90
  through decision-making, 5, 62-73
  through discipline, 5, 48-54
  through feelings of importance, 4,
    12-18
  through initiative, 24-26
  through knowledge of God's plan, 4,
    7-11
  through love, 4, 36-41
  through proper training, 5-6, 91-98
  through service, 4, 27-35
  through time with parents, 5, 55-61
Self-reliance, 24-26
Sermon on the Mount, 8
Service, anonymous, 32-33
  projects, 33-34
  self-esteem through, 4, 27-35
Sharing, 59
Sibling comparisons, 14-15, 38-39
Sibling rivalry, 32-33
Social interaction, opportunities for, 49
Social skills, 44-45
Spirit children, 3, 42
Stephen, forgiving spirit of, 9
Stephens, Evan, 68

— T —

Tantrums, 79-80
Tattling, 31
Television, 29-30, 58, 87-88
Temptation, resistance to, 11
Time, for children, 5, 55-61
  quality, 58, 61
"Time-out," 79-80
Tithing, 67
Traditions, family, 61
Training, self-esteem through, 5-6,
    91-98
  suggestions for, 95-97

— V —

Values, 67, 71, 72
Vindictiveness, 50
Vocation, choice of, 70-71

— W —

Welfare canneries, 33
Welfare farms, 33-34
Winning, 16-17
Work, made fun, 96-97
  simplification of, 97
  training children for, 94-98